STO

DITCHING

TRAINS

&

HIJACKING

AUTOMOBILES

true stories from the road less travelled

C. PÉTERS

Printed in the United States of America
First Printing, 2017
www.stoppingplanes.com

I have tried to recreate events, locales and conversations from my memories of them. Some names and identifying details have been changed to protect the privacy of individuals.

Illustrations by Flygohr, www.flygohr.com
Book production by Criss Ittermann
Editing by LeAnne, SpiderFly Agency
Cover and Book design by SpiderFly Agency

Ordering Information:

Quantity sales. Special discounts are available on quantity purchases by corporations, associations, and others. For details, please contact Christina Peters: christina@stoppingplanes.com or visit: www.stoppingplanes.com

"Travel is a journey that takes you farther than its destination."

Unknown

Dedication

I dedicate this book to you, dear reader. You.

This book is more than a love letter to travel.
It is more than an autobiography or an anthem of travel stories.
It is more than a cookbook.

Each story really happened.
To real people. Like you and me.

This book is proof that everything is possible.
How crazy wonderful real life is.
It is an invitation to become your own hero.
That loving life is the only way to be.

To carpe the diem and to maximize life.

PS. Don't use this as a road map. Tear it up and make your own.
Get lost and stay present.
The road less travelled is not a beaten path.
It is the one you have yet to discover.

I will tell you a little secret.
You will surprise yourself.
Of how awesome you are.

And how amazing this world is.

"I went into the woods because I wanted to live deliberately. I wanted to live deep and suck out all the marrow of life...to put out all that was not life; and not, when I came to die, discover I had not lived."

Henry Thoreau

TABLE OF CONTENTS

Gratitude

Thank you, Mom. For Everything.

Every story told here is true. And they are not all mine.
A huge thank you to each of you for sharing
your stories with me. With us all.

Pappa	Charley
Sally	Mark
Carolyn	Marek
Andy	Filippo
Fredrik	Ian
Janet	Unknown Soldier

I remember the first time you told me your stories.
I am still in awe. You are amazing.

I am a better person for knowing you, for your friendship.
Thank you.

This would not be possible without you. Thank you.
John & Patty, Jim & Deborah

You are not alone on the road less traveled. I definitely was not:
Mom, Pappa, Flygohr, Criss, Jake, Matt, Andy, Corey, Tony, Chris,
Emmanuelle, Fabienne, Ilse, Louise, Lyle, Riccardo, Guillemette,
Karen, Stefanie, Cassandra, Gunnar, Veronica, David, Alex, Fredrik,
Siv, Barnaby, Kia, Adele, Severine, Fred, Cecile, Fabrice, Mark,
Brian, Kate, Gail, Jesse, Bjorn, Emma, Nicole, Sara, George.

LAGNIAPPE

At the end of every chapter, there is "lagniappe", what
we call in New Orleans "a little extra": a local recipe to
try, along with a drink to enjoy, and music to listen to
(playlists are on Spotify under Stopping Planes).

Who says you need to get on a plane to travel?

Read. Drink. Eat. Dance. Enjoy.

Most of all, bon voyage.

"The question isn't 'who is going to let me?' It's 'who is going to stop me?'"

Ayn Rand

STOPPING PLANES
Nigeria

"Maybe these were not the right shoes to wear," I mumbled to myself, looking down at my high heels as I sat in the back of my taxi, racing along the back roads of Abuja.

I needed to get to the airport.

What I really needed was to get on a plane which was leaving in 20 minutes. And we were 25 minutes away. There might be some sprinting involved once we arrived at the departure hall.

But first things first: get to the airport.

Given there were no paved roads in the area, calling what we were rattling on a "back road" was flattering. It was a mixture of boulders, pot holes, dirt, sand, and the occasional road block. The underbelly of most cars cannot tolerate such abuse. That said, I was not worried about damage to the car.

Because calling the Flintstone automobile I was in "a car" was another overstatement. I half expected to look down and see the feet of my driver, George, moving rapidly on the ground, propelling us and the car towards the airport. The Flintstone mobile was a poor 1979 Renault which should have been abandoned in 1978. The color of the car was a dark hue of "rust". Its interior was made of plastic which would outlast future alien life on earth.

The rest of it, including the motor, was held together with chewing gum, wire, and twine. George had lifted the hood when we stopped for fill the tank with gas from the jerry can of fuel he had "bought" from the neighborhood Exxon pipeline. He wanted to give me confidence that we would get to the airport.

Confidence that the car actually worked. The air-conditioning not so much. Personally, I did not really care. Not wanting to pay the extra $20 for air-conditioning that did not work, I opted for au naturel air-conditioning, Nigerian style: wind together with sand, dust, and fumes. I could breathe, barely.

Which, of course, is the perfect environment to light a cigarette. Nothing like a moving Molotov cocktail. Feeling stressed, I lit one up and then exhaled. The health of my lungs was not my priority at that moment, surviving this taxi ride was. As was catching that plane.

I was determined and so was George. Bless his heart.

"Don't worry, Madame!" yelled George from the front. "Jesus will get us there!" He continued,"His angels have wings!" as he pointed to the bumper sticker on the dashboard that read: "Don't worry! Jesus is driving."

To prove his point, he took his hands off the wheel.

Oh, God.

In order for him to speak and peddle, George turned. And of course, the car turned with him. Almost into a ditch. To say that we were driving in a straight line was another overstatement.

"George!" I yelled. "Keep your eyes on the road. Jesus does not want me dead right now. Let's help the angels, shall we? And get there in one piece?"

George thought I was funny.

I wasn't joking.

I did laugh though. Shaking my head, I continued to smoke my cigarette, holding it with one hand while the other held the door in with twine. A feat for anyone being tossed like salad, trying to maintain balance while sitting in the back of Flintstone mobile. No matter. We rattled forward furiously. Finishing my cigarette, I stuck my head out the window for some air and inhaled fumes and dust.

Obviously, I was not worried about my lungs or my life for that matter. Molotov cocktail? Nah. I wasn't worried about that either. Nor the capability of George, his feet and his angels. I had to catch that plane. This might entail some running. Maybe some sprinting.

What was I worried about?

My shoes.

————

Earlier that morning, I had received my orders from my boss. Now, some bosses like to set goals. No, not him, not my boss. Calling the orders I received "a directive" would be suggesting that he was gentle. Uhm, no. He was pretty clear. I got orders and I had to follow them or else.

My "mission impossible" for the day was to get a contract signed by the Vice President of Nigeria. When would my boss like the contract signed? "Now," was the answer. Like now-now. Like yesterday. It would be difficult to misinterpret the urgency in his tone.

My orders were:
Step 1. Find the Vice President.
Step 2. Get him to sign the contract.
Easy. Peezy.

Exactly like that walk in the park that I took yesterday.

To start with, let's forget about the protocol of getting face time with the Vice President of a large, powerful African country. Let's also forget about the red tape to get this man to sign a contract on behalf of his country. Sounds easy, right?

There are few minor details, like this is someone I had never met. The second most powerful man in the country was not expecting me nor did he know anything about me. Nor my company. Nor my boss. Nor my newspaper. And let's just skip over the tiny details of entourage and security.

Forget about all that. Secondary details. Tiny.

First up was Step 1: to be in the same geographical location as the Vice President. This would help in achieving Step 2: getting through the entourage and security, obtaining some face time with the Vice President and successfully getting him to sign the contract.

You see, the Vice President was not in Abuja. He was not even in the same state. Where was he? He was in his hometown, his village, on the border of Chad. Far from where I was. Definitely not around the corner.

My boss handed me $200 for the plane ticket and hotel. He thought this would be enough to get his mission accomplished. Taking the money, I snapped my heels, saluted and was on my way.

———

Flashback two months. I had just signed up to be a journalist. No idea or inkling of what was going to happen to me or what I was going to live through. I signed up because I wanted to change the world, one word at a time, believing that the pen is mightier than the sword. I was going to be a glorious beacon of truth: a journalist. The greatest occupation ever.

Reality was a little different. It bites every once in awhile.

There was no school for this. I knew I had to be trained. I also knew there was a lot of work ahead; I welcomed it. However, the gentle internship I expected was a bit different from the reality: it was not so much an internship, but slavery. Whatever the boss wanted, he got. Forget about writing. My job was to fetch. The "beck and call" kind.

In other words, there was no nesting period. In this case, my boss cracked the egg open, threw me out of my comfort zone and told me to fly. The free fall was terrifying.

Funny what happens on the way down.

(You find your wings.)

Leaving his office, I went to quickly pack my bags, and left for the airport to book a ticket. Online booking agencies in Nigeria do not exist. Neither do travel agencies in Abuja, for that matter. If you wanted to fly, you had to be physically at the airport and buy the ticket there, on the spot. It would not be advisable to buy tickets from anyone else in town because tickets were literally pieces of paper with some chicken scratch on them. Anyone, literally anyone, could create a fake ticket. The only differentiator was the "chop", the official stamp of the airline on your ticket. If it was not stamped, your ticket was not valid.

It is important to make clear that in order to clamp down on fraud, the airlines only kept one stamp, one "chop". And this stamp was always at the airport.

So, off to the airport I went. I knew that there were three flights to the Vice President's hometown that day. And the first one was leaving in three hours. With time to spare, I got my first taxi of the day to the airport. Making good time, I practically waltzed up to the ticket desk.

However, to my immediate dismay, the first flight at 9.30 a.m. was already fully booked. Ok. Sigh of initial frustration. One flight down. There are two more. "Not a problem," I told myself.

Turning to the lady behind the desk, I asked, "When is the next flight?"

"When God wants," she answered, not even bothering to look up. Ok. I knew what this meant; I was going to have to be patient. In capital letters. The ticket lady had "the chop" and therefore all the power. She proceeded to ignore me for 20 minutes, choosing instead to make tea, catch up on some family gossip, braiding her assistant's hair, while chatting as if I was not there.

I was tempted to ask if she needed a break from all her "busy - ness", but kept my mouth shut. I knew how important patience is, no matter where you are from. This was one of those times.

Instead, I took the time to inhale the aroma of a fully packed airport of bustling Nigerians. Women dressed in every color, with headdresses that nearly reached the ceiling fan, tempting death by strangulation. Most men were businessmen in a uniform of shiny polyester suits, fake Rolexes, and gator skin dress shoes. There were also young men in whitewashed jeans and hand-me-down t-shirts, selling soda pop, water, and chewing gum. Everyone was hustling. I bought a coke and a smile, enjoying the drink as much as I did joking around with them.

On the sidelines were the toy soldiers of the Nigerian Army, leaning against the ticket desks while they flirted with the sales ladies. You could spot them anywhere: all dressed in black uniforms with matching berets. Each had his own gun. I imagine that they were there for airport security. How efficient they were, I could not guess. For one, they were kids. These soldiers had faces that were too young for shave. And I doubt that they had any professional training even in holding a gun. They dragged the guns behind them on the floor.

I am sure that the safety on their guns was on. Positive.

Finally, the "chop master" decided to grace me with an answer after I had been waiting for almost a half an hour.

"11.30 a.m." she told me. "But you cannot buy it now."

"Why?" I asked.

"I do not have the appropriate paper to print tickets," my friendly ticket Nazi replied. "Come back and I will sell you."

You have got to be kidding. She made me wait for more than twenty minutes to tell me that she had the stamp but not the paper.

"Ok," I sighed to myself. Let's make lemonade out of lemons. Instead of wasting time at the airport, I could use the time effectively and impress my boss with getting a few errands done in town. There was enough time to go and come back.

Decision made, I started weaving my way through the throng

at the airport, catching another taxi back into town. Less than an hour later, I was back at the airport, standing in front my new "best friend".

Ms. Ticket Nazi looked up and sighed.

"No more tickets," she said.

"What!!! What do you mean?" I could not believe it.

"The Governor bought all tickets." She was looking at me as if I should have known.

"No way. Impossible." Looking down at my feet, which were hurting from all this running around, I doubled down and was resolved to be sweet. Sweetness and light was the only way I was going to convince this woman to sell me a ticket. And when that didn't work, money always talked.

"How much for the next ticket at 1.30 p.m.?" I asked.

"$120. It is the last flight." she replied.

"What! The ticket is usually $40 one way!" I knew I was going to have to pay but not that much. $10 or $20 would get me far. $100 was over and above the call of duty.

Besides, I only had $200 for the entire trip.

I knew I was in trouble. There was no way I could go back to the "or else" of my boss. So, I bought the ticket. I had $60 left. Actually, I had $40. I was going to have to walk home on $40 dollars. Walk home from the border of Chad and Nigeria. Because this was a one way ticket.

"No stress," I told myself. I could go home, get cash, and be back before the flight left in 2 hours time. It would be rushed, but I am sure that it was manageable. Besides, I needed the money.

Making my decision, off I went to find a taxi - my fourth of the day. And of course, all the taxis were gone. Except for a tiny tin can belonging to a man called George.

"Do you want air conditioning?" he asked.

"No, thank you," I replied and rolled down the window.

Little did I know...

———

Of course, there was no cash at home or in the office. Why would there be? Murphy is not only a law, it is my personal "constitution".

I got back in the car, sat down on the plastic seat, sighed and covered my face with my hands. I had to make a choice. Go large or go home.

George turned to look at me, "Where do you want to go, Madame?"

"Back to the airport, George. I am getting that flight."

Go large it was. All chips were in.

No one was going to be "or else" to me, boss or not. I was getting that plane, that contract, that respect. If I had to crawl back from Chad. I was going to make it happen.

Off we went. Rattling, peddling, racing the rust bucket back to the airport, George was praying out loud to the angels and I was wondering if it was a good time to light a cigarette. I began to bargain with myself: the fumes were not that noticeable with the window down, but I could still smell gas despite inhaling all the sand. Cigarette or life? Priorities, schmorities.

Deciding to deep breathe with my head out the window, I joined George in prayer. This time I was praying to the "time gods", or whoever is in charge of time. I was humbly asking for a few extra seconds or minutes. I was not asking for much. Just time.

But time waits for no man, or woman for that matter. I think the angels had to choose between stopping time or getting me to the airport alive. (Not that they normally don't have their hands full.)

We pulled up to the airport. I was ready to jump out when George tapped my arm, "I will wait here for you, Madame. Don't worry. I will take you home if you do not make your flight."

I love this man. My compadre. My Flintstone Jesus. He was so sweet.

"Thank you, George. But I am getting on," I replied. I hugged him, gave him almost all the cash I had and started running.

It was 1.30 p.m. I thought to myself, nothing leaves on time in Nigeria. Everything runs on Africa time. I have at least 20 minutes.

Sprinting through the airport in my high heels, dragging my suitcase behind me, weaving between the turbans, the hustlers, the suitcases. "Excuse me, Pardon me," I murmured as I pushed through the throng of bodies between me and the gate.

I thought I had time. Um, no. Apparently, I did not. When I got to the gate, panting and heaving deep breaths, Ms. Chop Nazi greeted me, smiling a smile that would make crocodiles jealous.

"The gate is closed. You cannot go. Look, the plane has already started to leave. It is on the runway."

I do not know why she seemed pleased. I did not care. She just told me that the gate was closed and that the flight was on its way.

I looked out the door. And sure enough, the plane was taxiing down the runway.

"Oh no, you don't. You are not leaving."

"You" being the plane, of course.

Pushing her aside, I barged through the platoon of teenage soldiers guarding the door, jumping over their AK 47s on the ground, and started to run out onto the runway.

I think that was the time when all hell broke loose. Oh, my. There was screaming. I heard it but paid it no mind. I was running for my life. Chop Nazi was too large to move but not so for the toy soldiers. They were in better shape. They had alerted their command that a crazy woman was on the tarmac, running to meet the plane head on.

(I think they thought I was crazy, even called me that on their walkie-talkies. But I assure you, dear reader, I was perfectly sane. Still am.)

I was going to get that plane.

Truth be told, if anything was going to stop me, it was going to be these damn high heels. No matter, I could run barefoot. And walk back from Chad, barefoot too.

Nothing was not going to stop me: not the heels, not the Nigerian army, not Chop Nazi, not Murphy's law, not the clock, and definitely not this plane.

What was my plan, you ask? My plan was that I had no plan. Nope. None. Just focus. Just the plane. Get to the plane. Meet it on the runway. And then figure it out from there. I needed to get on the plane, not just catch it.

There was only one thing that could stop me. Bullets. I needed to outrun the Nigerian army boys who were closing in. I could hear them, screaming after me. Thank god they did not know how to run and lock and load, much less shoot.

Guess what happened next?

Wonder of wonders, the plane began to slow to a stop.

The 747 stopped. Right in front of me.

Unbelievable. It stopped taking off.

I was in awe.

I came to an abrupt halt, too. Of course. Struck and amazed.

In less than a second, one of the soldiers grabbed my arm. I felt the same pressure on the other arm. They were not too happy. Actually, they were a bit upset. Maybe more than upset. Kind of angry.

I turned to them and said, dripping in my Southern drawl, "Thank you for escorting me, gentlemen. You are too kind."

I do not know what they said in return. I speak Pidgin not Hausa, but to be fair, I could not hear a word they were saying since the airplane's wind turbines were deafening. Any intent to listen to them was forgotten as soon as I saw the plane's door open and the ramp coming down.

"Yes!" I tried to fist pump but the soldiers were holding me. Standing at the door of the plane, the pilot yelled at the soldiers to let me go. And they did. With a dropped jaw, I began to climb the stairs.

Oh man, this was incredible. I could not believe what had just happened. Correct that - what was still happening - as I walked up the stairs and boarded the plane. With no lack of drama in my life, I turned to the soldiers and blew them kisses. I even waved goodbye to Chop Nazi, because I am classy like that.

Ducking my head, I entered the plane. The sound of the wind turbines was now muted by the tirade of the pilot telling me off. And as I turned to find my seat, I heard another sound: clapping and cheering.

It was the passengers. All of them. They were standing up and cheering for me. Every single one. Of course, I curtsied. And took an encore with a bow. It was as if a rock star had entered the plane. Not being one, I began to be just a little bit conscious of my disheveled appearance, sand crusted hair and face and sweat stains. Well, at least the high heels were good for something.

The passengers had seen the entire episode from their windows. They were the ones who had pleaded with the pilot and insisted he stop the plane.

Blowing kisses and thanking them, even shaking hands with a few, I limped down the aisle to my seat. One of them wanted to hug me. I was like a celebrity. Another reached out to help me with my suitcase. I smiled, thankful for his help.

It was an incredible moment. A "once in a lifetime" event in life I will never forget. I knew that then, when I found my seat, and I know it now.

Exhaling, I sat down and pushed my chair back in a recline.

Looking out of my window, as the plane began to taxi off again, I proceeded to kick off my shoes. My feet were tingling. Hell, I was tingling. With surreal excitement.

I made it.

Step 1:
I got on the plane. Check.
$10 left. Check.
No bullet holes. Check.
No hotel room for tonight. Check.
No return flight for tomorrow. Check.
No food. Check.

What next? Step 2?

I smiled.

What "next" is bring it on.

Bring it all on.

═══════════

─────────

P.S. I did get that contract signed. By the Vice President the next day. And I did get home. Via Chad. But that is for another story, another chapter. Let's call it: Step 2…

Lagniappe

I had cold soda that day. Fanta to be precise. However, with beef suya, nothing is better than cold beer. It is a perfect match.

For this chapter, I chose one of my favorite Nigerian dishes: Beef Suya. You can find it sold on almost every street corner; it is a perfect snack for anyone in a rush. It is easy to make and very good.

Beef Suya

40 minutes

Grill Medium or Oven: 250°C/375°F

1 kg beef or chicken
5 tbsp. suya spice
2 cubes of meat stock (ex. Knorr)
½ tsp. salt
ground dried pepper
grill sticks
vegetable oil

1. Cut beef/chicken/meat into thin fillets of beef or square if chicken.
2. Mix 5 spoons of suya spice with ground cubes of Knorr, salt and ground pepper.
3. Sprinkle the seasoning over the meat, on both sides.
4. Stake the meat, brush them with vegetable oil, sprinkle again.
5. Place on hot grill.
6. Turn every 10 minutes for 40 minutes; Apply spices half way through.

Done. Together with a nice cold beer, this dish is sublime.

"Stay thirsty, my friends."

Dos Equis advertising campaign

WHOREHOUSE HERO

Mexico

"Pizza?" my father asks one evening, "You feel like it?"
"I am starving," my brother replies. "Tina? You coming?"

As if they did not know the answer. It is always yes. And today it was: hell, yeah. You see, I am easy to please. All you have to say are the magic words: pizza. And if you add the words: 'double helping of pepperoni' and 'ice cold beer', I will put down whatever I am doing and follow you out the door to the restaurant.

Which is exactly what I did.

Now, normally, eating pizza with your family would not qualify as a story worth retelling. However, this is not just any story. This particular evening was different. Therefore, it is important that I set the scene. Not just for tale, but for the telling of it.

To start off, the story takes place in Mexico and it is about a whorehouse that gets shot up and about the hero that saves the day.

But why is the telling of the story so important? And why is this story is so different than the rest?

Let me help you, dear reader.

The story is in the details.

You see, it is my father who is the hero in the whorehouse...

––––––––––

We went to the local Albanian pizzeria around the corner, the kind of restaurant that has Christmas lights flashing all year round to give that particular "romantic" glow. The tables are covered with red-checked plastic tablecloths. Eros Ramazzotti croons on repeat. There are candles everywhere for extra effect, all of them battery operated, flickering in tandem with the Christmas lights. What can I say? It was a classy joint.

The owner of said establishment was more Michelin Man than Michelin Star. His name was Tito. After he left Albania 10 years ago, he spent 6 months in Milan learning how to cook. He claims this is where he learned how to make pizza. I could vouch for him; Tito was truly talented. I don't know if it was Italian pizza, but it was good.

In fact, we liked it so much, we ate there all the time. Coming to Tito's restaurant is like coming home, eating your favorite food with no clean up. Bonus: Tito had an open bar for his favorite customers. This would naturally invite longs nights of discussion and partying until all the liquor behind the bar was drunk and all the stories were told. In short, we lived at Tito's and slept at home.

Anyway, once upon a time - last year in fact - we were sitting together after the meal. The wine bottles were empty and the Tito's Albanian moonshine was out.

Now, my father likes to talk about the "golden days", as I imagine every old man does. And like every daughter or son can attest, we have heard these stories a thousand times. Every Christmas. And again on Easter. And don't forget birthdays.

I can repeat word for word every story my father has ever told.

But not this one. Not this time.

On this particular evening, I had already settled in, prepared to hear the same story for the thousandth time. Sober might not be the option for story #1001. My glass was full of Albanian moonshine and I was practicing my Italian with Tito. Actually, it was more like singing since we knew all Eros' lyrics by heart.

All of a sudden, through the noise and singing, my ears picked up "Acapulco".

My father was talking. And he was telling a story that took place in the mountains above Acapulco.

Hmm.

This was not expected. I did not know of any story that took place there.

Confused, I turned to my father.

"Acapulco? When were you in Acapulco?"

"1968. Before I met your mother," he replied.

"Ahhh. What happened?"

Now, dear reader, this is when someone should have taken the moonshine out of my hands and told me to "buckle up, cowgirl!" Even a tiny warning would have been nice. Because I had no idea what was coming.

"It is the time I got shot up in a whorehouse," he told me with a straight face.

Whorehouse? Shot up? In it? Que?

"What!?" I sputtered Tito's moonshine all over the table.

I knew I had heard him correctly. Strange, right?

"But I didn't get shot," he said, as reaching over to clap my hand, a gesture that meant that I should not worry.

Of course I was comforted.

As if someone had thrown a bucket of cold water all over me.

"What were you doing in a whorehouse?" The minute I asked that question, I knew it was rhetorical.

My brother started with, "Well, Christina, there are the birds and the bees...."

"Cute, real cute," I countered. I congratulated my brother on truly original banter, before turning back to Dad for more information.

I raised my eyebrows in question, "Pappa?"

With a look of complete innocence, my father said, "I was there for water. I did not know it was a whorehouse. I got lost in Acapulco and was thirsty. So, I stopped at this place for water."

"You got lost?" I shook my head in disbelief. This is my father who taught me how to navigate using the North Star. As long as I have known him, he has never gotten lost. In fact, many call him the "walking GPS". And now he is telling me he got lost searching for water.

Dumbstruck, I look at him as he flirts with the pretty waitress while she pours him another glass of Tito's moonshine.

Lost?

Water?

My ass.

———

Refills all round. Tito was not moving; he wanted to hear the story as much as I did. My brother was laughing at me. I thought that no matter what I had just heard, it was going to get better or more significant.

Like a crack in the earth right before a canyon forms.

That kind of significant.

Leaving the military service in Sweden as a Navy officer, my father went to Buenas Aires to practice law. (Why? I have no idea. He spoke 6 languages. Por que no? Argentina was a good place to start as any I suppose. Especially if you have adventure in your blood.) And after a year in Buenas, he decided to go to the U.S. and further his education in management at Berkeley.

For many, the obvious route to get to San Francisco from Buenas Aires would be to fly right? Not so for my father. Choosing a more scenic route, he took a one way flight to Mexico City, where he bought a car to drive all the way to Las Vegas, via Acapulco.

Because Acapulco is on the way.

And Berkeley's campus is in Vegas.

Not.

 I was beginning to get a clue of the kind of further education he was interested in. And it wasn't law.

"I loved that car. It was the sweetest car. The Camaro. Beautiful with a black racing stripe down the front. It was such a great ride." My father was mourning his car, similar to a salute given to a fallen soldier before recounting an ancient battle.

I didn't care about the car. Why was he talking about the car? I wanted to know about the water. What was my father doing in a whorehouse in Acapulco? How did he get there?

Finishing his glass, he started his story with dramatic pauses. His audience definitely was engaged. I was on the edge of my seat.

"I was driving up this dusty road, windows down, and needed to stop for water."

In my head the movie started: I could imagine the heat, the dust, the mountains overlooking the city Acapulco and the azure waters, teasing the white sands. I could imagine his white Camaro (with the black stripe) racing up the mountain, dust from the road stirring clouds in the wake.

I could hear The Monkees on the radio, his hand tapping to the beat on the side of the car with the windows down. And then, I see my father shift gears, as he drives slowly through the town, its main street lined with small buildings and one story houses.

He is wearing a crisp white shirt, a cravat around his neck, cufflinks at his wrists and pressed dress pants. Sunglasses were on. He is the European debonair. (How do I know this? Because his uniform has never changed. To this day, he wears the same thing. He rarely wears ties, always preferring to wear a cravat. He also does not own a pair of jeans. I kid you not. My father does not own a pair of jeans.)

I see him coming to a stop, parking, and then leaving the car, closing the door with a swoosh. Turning towards the building, he smiles at the sun and readjusts his sunglasses while he walks towards the swinging doors.

Halt. My movie is incomplete. I am missing information. What was the sign outside the building? And why stop there? Who looks for water at a whorehouse?

"Dad, did you know it was a whorehouse?"

He shook his head. Was that a "no"? Because I did not hear a "yes". Are there no 7/11s in Mexico? Call me crazy, but I do not think that most Mexicans go to whorehouses for their water.

I imagined my father walking towards a sun washed building, similar to those in a Mexican Western movie, complete with swinging, slated wooden doors. Entering the establishment, you first come across a long bar with stools, empty and waiting. There is the stereotypical barman standing behind the counter, bored out of his mind playing with a toothpick in his mouth. Mirrored shelves behind him, stocked with alcohol, bottles of all sizes and color. The barman is drinking straight from the tequila bottle before serving the solitary customer.

I imagine he is probably waiting for his turn; business must be good.

To the left of the bar are sofas covered with red velvet, worn to a dusky pink. Tattered golden tassels decorate the cushions. The same tassels also hang from the heavy red velvet curtains, now drawn to keep out the light. Permanently. However, every once in a while, the sun escapes spotlighting the action on the sofa.

There are other curtains, but those are beaded. They rattle as every client passes through en route to back of the house, and then again when they returned satisfied before stopping at the bar to pay.

There is one fan in the room. Mounted on the ceiling. Covered with dust. It looks like it started and stopped working on the same day it was bought years ago. Every once in a while, the fan rotates once, as if in jest.

Someone should try to fix it. Because it is hot and it is sweaty.

In my mind's eye, I see couples on the sofa. One couple is a working girl sitting on her patron's lap. Cowboy hat resting next to him, he is in varying degrees of undress: his shirt is long gone and his pants are undone. At the ankles. The woman however is naked. And giggling. And moaning. Their sounds intermingles with the music of the mariachis coming from the radio.

With the doors swinging behind him, my father enters the establishment. He takes it all in before sitting on one of the bar stools. Swiveling to the barman, he asks for "water".

Of course you did, Dad.

"We had an excellent conversation, the bartender and I. It lasted for hours." My father turns to me and says, "We were not drinking water."

"Yeah, Dad. I guessed as much."

He grins and confesses, "I got a little tipsy."

"It was such a wonderful conversation, I could not say no to the lovely women that were there either. I can never say no. How can you say no to such beauty?" He says this as he turns to the waitress, kisses her hand and asks for more of Tito's Albanian special brew.

She giggles.
I roll my eyes. He is getting into character.
And the character is him.

"The men were very interesting, too."

Oh, I am sure, Dad. In my movie, I am not sure if he is on the bar stool, on the sofa, or in the back room. But for my sanity, he is still on the bar stool.

He continues, "I must have been there for several hours,

drinking, enjoying it all. Great conversation. The barman was incredible.

And then all of a sudden, these two men came into the whore-house and started shooting up the place."

"What! What did you say?!" I sobered quickly.

Yes, they had guns. Machine guns. And they started shooting it up. Everything. Bullets were flying everywhere."

I see the bullets flying in slow motion, in all directions, whistling through the air. Hitting the mirrored glass, sending shards everywhere, raining over the bartender who is crouching on the ground behind the bar. I see the bullets hit the sofa with a thud, with feathers flying in the air, finally released from their velvet confinement. I see bullets hitting the fan, spinning it into motion, probably for the second time since its birth. I see naked women screaming, covering their heads. Breasts everywhere. I see the men, shuffling with their pants around their legs, grabbing their cowboy hats to cover their heads or their prized possessions, not knowing which one is more precious. I see. Complete chaos.

Knowing my father has never been shot, something did not make sense.

I had to interrupt him to ask, "And you? What happened to you, Dad?"

"I didn't move," he replied with absolute sincerity.

Shaking my head, I repeated, "You did not move? In the entire shoot up? With bullets flying everywhere?

"No."

"I stayed on the bar stool and did not budge."

"You are kidding."

"No."

"You did not move the entire time? With bullets flying everywhere? Not at all?"

"No", he said.

My jaw went slack.

Awesome.

I re-imagined my entire movie, with bullets whizzing everywhere, hitting the glass, moving the ceiling fan, with screaming working women, and shuffling patrons in the heat, in the sweat, breaking up the moans with piercing the sounds of guns shattering, clicking and reloading. I see breasts, cowboy hats, flying feathers, shards of wood splintering.

And then my father in the midst of it, untouched and unmoving in his crisp white shirt, silk cravat, lifting his drink to his lips, and the light reflecting off his cufflinks.

Incredible. Unbelievable.

And awesome.

Tito started clapping. I lifted my glass. Well, not really. I wanted to but I was too shocked.

I kept on thinking, 'Wow. He is better than any movie. This is amazing.'

"Did anybody die?" Look at me, asking about the gore.

"No," he said, clapping the top of my hand again. "Nobody died. The place was a mess though. It was destroyed."

I was relieved. But still curious. "So, what happened?"

"I helped them clean up," he answered. I was expecting a different answer, maybe that he would make calls to the police and the hospital. But no, he was "helping them clean up".

Something did not sound right. You see, my father hates to clean. He is not housebroken now and he was definitely was not in 1968.

"How did you do that?"

"Well, I helped with the ladies, of course." Of course. His

40

version of "cleaning up" is helping with the ladies, the working women.

The naked working women.

"Everyone was completely amazed. I became a hero because I did not move. Everyone thought I was amazing. We had just escaped death. And I wanted to comfort the ladies. They were distraught. So, I thought we should continue the party and leave the cleaning to another day."

My father was proud. Of his humanitarian gesture.

I was still curious. Details, right? "So, what did you do?"

"Well, the only normal thing to do. I took everyone to the whorehouse down the street," he replied in the same tone as if I had asked him what was 1+1.

"You did what?"

"I took the ladies to the whorehouse down the street. With a brush of death like that, we wanted to party. It was the obvious thing to do."

"You took whores to a whorehouse?" I asked. I had to be sure that I had heard him correctly. Because everything else seemed completely normal.

Not.

"Yes." he nodded, emptying his drink with a smile.

"You are the only man that takes whores to a whorehouse."

"You are a whorehouse hero," I said, while shaking my head in disbelief.

That he was.

In my mind's eye, the movie comes to an end, with the sun setting in the background; the sky saturated with orange, pink and red.

The dirt road is center screen, lined with the houses on either side. It is quiet, with the exception of the small parade of a couple dozen people making its way down the main street.

The camera focuses on my father, the tall Swedish debonair, with his arms around three scantily dressed women, one of them wearing a cowboy hat with bullet holes in it. Their colleagues and patrons follow him, two by two, in couple format. Some are wearing clothes. Some not so much.

The bartender pulls up the rear, clasping a bottle to his chest. He occasionally stops to take large swigs of tequila, a needed fortification in order to process his recent brush with death.

As a true gentleman, my father stops at the entrance of the establishment, and holds the door open for the women and men to enter. The music beckons. And as they pass him, the women kiss him on the mouth and the men clap him on the back, shaking his hand. The bartender hugs him.

Once everyone is in, he smiles at the women who are pulling on his hands to follow them inside. But just before he enters through the swinging doors himself, he pauses and turns to the camera.

And winks.

═══════════

Lagniappe

Feel free to have red wine, as I did, when listening to this story the first time. Or have a cold beer, the beverage of choice at the whorehouse. Or if you can find it, try a glass of Albanian moonshine.

I would say water, but you know where that gets you...

Since I do not think that whorehouses or bordellos have working kitchens, it was difficult to think of just one dish which would suit the story. So I chose two: salsa and pizza. Claro.

Salsa
5 minutes. Nada màs.

4 Roma tomatoes, cored and quartered
1 to 2 serrano chiles, stemmed, seeded, and sliced
Juice of 1 to 2 limes
1 teaspoon coarse salt
½ teaspoon freshly ground pepper

1. Pour into blender and puree until it is smooth. That is it. Done.

Pizza
45 minutes

Oven: 400°F for 20 minutes

I am a big fan of ordering in but here goes if you decide to make pizza at home. Some people are very talented at this; I am not one of them, since I never seem to get the crust right. (Which is probably a good thing, like not knowing how to make chocolate.)

Part I - Crust
2½ cups of flour
1 teaspoon salt
1 teaspoon sugar
1 tablespoon fast rise yeast
1 cup water
1 tablespoon oil

1. In large bowl, mix everything EXCEPT water and oil.
2. After mixed, then add water and oil.
3. Turn onto floured surface; knead for 2 minutes.
4. Place in a greased bowl; turning to grease top.
5. Cover and let rise for 20 minutes.
6. Punch down; place on 12 inch, greased pizza pan.
7. Pat into a circle.

Part II - Topping

¼ cup tomato sauce
1 teaspoon italian seasoning
½ teaspoon garlic powder
½ teaspoon salt
⅛ teaspoon pepper
1½ cups pepperoni slices
1 cup shredded monterey jack cheese
1 cup shredded mozzarella cheese
3 tablespoons grated parmesan cheese

1. Mix everything EXCEPT cheeses and pepperoni.
2. Spread mixture over crust.
3. Place half of pepperoni on top.
4. Sprinkle half of cheeses on top.
5. Place rest of pepperoni on top of cheeses.
6. Sprinkle the rest of the cheeses (and add more for good luck).
7. Bake at 400 for 20 minutes until light brown.

Seriously, you can live happily ever after just knowing how to make these two dishes.

"**Do not take life too seriously, you will never get out alive.**"

Elbert Hubbard

Scotch-Taped Planes

Russia

I like to tell this story to people that I meet who are afraid of flying. Everyone should know about how to go down in flames.

———

Chewing gum ought to do it, I thought to myself. It was like there was a screw loose somewhere on the plane. It was causing this irritating clinking of metal which was sending me up the wall, and the incessant rattling was getting on my nerves.

Pop. A few more chews. I took it out of my mouth and stuck it on the overhead bin. This was a double bonus because now the oxygen mask was no longer flapping in my face.

I did not think I would need it later. Little did I know...

I should have known that there was more than one screw loose on this plane flying from Minsk to Moscow. The give-away when we boarded should have been that all the oxygen masks were hanging down. Every single one of them. The other give-away should have been that the majority of passengers were drunk, from fear of flying. Russians never strike me as being fearful. They always seem to be prepared. Winter hardened. Unphased. I mean, they bring guns to their discos. Now, I see they bring vodka to their flights.

Ok, then. Maybe I should strap in for this one.

Smiling politely at my neighbors as I tightened my seat belt, the man across the aisle responded by reaching over to offer me a cigarette and a swig of his vodka bottle. I took both.

Yes, ladies and gentlemen, we were smoking on the plane. In the olden golden days when smoking was allowed on aircrafts, non-smokers were in the front of the plane and the smokers would be in the back. The thought was that this division would not disturb the non-smoking passengers, as the fans would push the smoke to the back of the plane.

However, not here. Not on this plane. Not in Russia. This particular aircraft had a different method. Smokers and non-smokers were split down the middle. On the left were the smokers and on the right were the non-smokers. Whoever designed this formula was definitely not following the laws of physics.

Seconds after lighting my cigarette, the stewardess saw me smoking and was not happy. Tapping on my shoulder, she informed me that I had to change seats. Because I was violating the rules. I was on the wrong side of the plane. I was told to change seats and sit next to the man who had given me the smoke and the swig. I got up to sit next to my 'supplier' and squeezed into whatever was left of the seat. (He was not a small man.)

After getting as comfortable as I could, Mr. Marlboro Man smiled and offered me another cigarette and another swig of his vodka bottle. Sweet. He speaks my kind of language. Not bad. The next thirty minutes was a series of raising our bottle to give pause to the random conversation we were "having". Where neither party understood the other.

Besides "da" and "niet", I actually have no idea what he was talking about. But we got along famously, as we continued to "smoke vodka and down cigarettes".

Suddenly, the plane began to waver. Now, when I say waver, I mean it was not flying in a straight line. Turbulence would be the polite term. The overhead lights went on as the pilot told us over the loudspeaker: "buckle up and stay seated".

The plane began to rattle. I am guessing it was all the loose screws in this flying tin can. Then the oxygen masks began to swing. In fact, I think a seat or two moving, lifting off the floor. I remember thinking to myself, instead of getting cheap on screws, maybe they should nail down those seats.

But, you know what, I could be hallucinating this. I could hardly see for the smoke of the cigarettes. (Remember, dear reader, it was not just me smoking but half of the plane's passengers as well. All whom were seated on the left side of course.)

You also need to know that my eyesight after 7 or 8 shots of vodka is not what it used to be.

I told myself to be calm because the plane is perfectly fine. And that the annoying oxygen mask flapping in my face every single time the plane moved was nothing to worry about. That and the view from my window: a not-so-insignificant trail of smoke streaming from what could be called, the plane's engine.

Don't worry. Be happy.

While I was talking myself out of a panic attack, Mr. Marlboro Man had a different reaction. He was entertained. He loved this. He took a swig of the bottle, to clear his throat before he began to hum a song under his breath. A few seconds later, the volume has increased to full Pavarotti.

He was singing with all his heart. And so, when in "Rome", the story goes...I chirped in. Since I do not know any Russian songs, I chose an anthem of my own and started humming a Backstreet Boy song. (Don't judge me. I love Backstreet Boys, and if I decide to sing their song while tumbling out of the sky in a tin can on fire - that is my prerogative.)

Other people sing hymns. I know my mother would. Some people might sing their national anthem. In fact, I think that is what my neighbor started singing. Or it could be a Russian lullaby. It all sounded the same to me.

Before long, we were not the only ones singing. The entire plane was singing together, smokers and non-smokers united, swaying with the song, while the oxygen masks kept tempo.

It was rousing. I got chills. I almost handed in my passport and asked for a Russian one. My heart was stirred. Not by fear but by passion. Because of the song. Or it could be the vodka.

As the song finished, we all cheered, clapped, and drank from our bottles. Nobody was sitting down anymore because first we had all stood to sing the song, like a salute. And now, we were vigorously hugging each other.

I got two wet kisses on both cheeks from Mr. Marlboro Man. And then I reached over the seat to hug and kiss our neighbors in front of us.

It was a love fest. Everyone was emotional. It was like the plane had turned into a karaoke bar right before closing time, when people are gushing to each other, "I love you, man."

The stewardess had given up trying to seat us. They were buckled in. The pilot, on the loudspeaker, continued to ask everyone to sit down. To no avail.

A moment of sobriety hit and I wondered why we were all clapping and hugging and kissing.

Ah, that's right. Last rites. The plane was going down.

What a way to go.

What a way to die.

What a time to be alive.

Lagniappe

Of course, you are going to drink vodka with this story. Ice is optional. Tea is not allowed.

Personally, I like my vodka straight, without food. But if you are hungry, you are in for a treat because here comes one of the most traditional foods of the Russian cuisine: blinis.

I have been told that blinis are not pancakes. I am confused. They look like them, act like them but are not them. Apparently, you are not allowed to add maple syrup to these bad boys. It does not mean that they are not sweet. Some are sweet and some are not. You can have them however you like: with butter and jam, or creme fraiche and salmon.

Blinis

2 eggs
1 tablespoon white sugar
⅓ teaspoon salt
½ cup all-purpose flour
2 ½ cups milk
1 tablespoon softened butter

1. Mix the dry.

2. Then mix the wet.

3. Then combine the two.

4. The batter should be thin.

5. Over hot griddle or pan, pour 2 tablespoons of batter.

6. Flip when edges are crisp and bubbles have formed. 1 more minute and then you are done.

7. After each blini is done, add a smidgen of butter.

8. Serve salty or sweet. Powdered sugar and jam or creme fraiche and salmon bites. And of course, caviar. When in Rome…

Note: If you are looking for something else to have with your vodka, try marinated herring and black bread with chopped raw onions (for extra taste).

"People come into your life for a reason, a season, or a lifetime."

Unknown

A FRUITFUL CONVERSATION

Cuba

Sigh. Not again. Lost.

"Are you kidding me? How are you lost again?" Mumbling, I was berating myself. It is not as if I did not often drive to Havana, either during the week for work or for fun. This time I was returning to Varadero from a weekend of fun.

And everyone knows the kind of fun you have in the beginning of the month when you get paid. Good times. Good times. So, I was literally living the great life in Cuba for several months as an executive for a hotel in Varadero. My first job. And in Cuba.

Who could ask for more? Great job, beautiful country, amazing experiences, paid in U.S. dollars. I even had a car, a brand new BMW with CD player which worked. With full surround sound. This was the good life: driving through the country, listening to music on the way back to Varadero, whizzing by fields and people walking on the side of the highway.

But now I was lost. I had absolutely no idea where I was going or where I was. And of course, I had no map.

"Stupid," I muttered to myself.

What to do? The best option is to ask for help from a local. It must be said that help is easily found in Cuba. People are happy to help. However, there might be a small exchange to be made. The last time I got lost, I asked for directions from someone on the side of the road. I ended up driving my guide to his village, which was the opposite side of Varadero. Nothing like a tour of Cuba by car. (Good thing Cuba is an island.)

So, this time I was a little wary about asking for help. Up ahead, there was an elderly man pushing a fruit cart. "Perfect," I thought to myself. He might be willing to help and probably will not need a ride.

I stopped along the side of the road, rolled down my window and leaned over to ask for directions. The elderly gentleman put down the cart, wiped his brow, put his hat back on and walked over to the side of the car.

"Que quieres?" (What do you want?) he asked.

"Direcciones por Varadero, por favor," I replied. (Directions for Varadero, please.)

He rattled them off quickly in Spanish. Varadero was not far as I had thought. It seems that I was not so lost, which was great. I was relieved that I now knew how to get home.

The friendly fruit vendor finished giving directions, to which I responded with a nod of gratitude, "Muchas gracias" (Thank you).

I began to turn the wheel to leave, now knowing where to go.

As soon as the car started to move, the elderly Cuban grabbed the window ledge of the car and smiling, leaned in to ask:

"No tienes algo para mi?" (Do you not have anything for me?)

Of course. Of course, I did. I had just gotten paid and had the envelope of cash on me, all $2,500 in $20 bills. I pulled out a bill and reached over to give it to him. He took the bill and started to walk back to his cart, as he thanked me, "Muchas gracias".

I will push pause on telling this story in order to give you some background. I knew that the average wages per month in the hotel industry was $300. However, after the 90% taxes and fees, the take home per month was $30. So, if someone in the hotel industry took home $30 per month, the question is: how much did a fruit farmer take home, if he sold his wares on the side of the road? It wouldn't be a lot. I cannot imagine when this man had last seen a $20 bill.

Back to the story.

———————

Having given him the money, I made moves to start the car again.

It took a split second for the fruit farmer to realize the amount of money he had in his hand. He rushed back to the car. His relaxed demeanor had turned into an intense look of heroism and an intense look of something else - of what I did not know and was yet to discover.

"No crees que lo dicen. Es todo en mentida," he told me. (Do not believe what they tell you. They are all lies.)

"What?" I am thinking: Where did this come from? Why is he telling me this? I was in the car, transfixed by this elderly farmer and the outpouring of his heart.

As he continued to speak, I started to calculate his age. He seemed to be at least 65. He was old enough to have lived through the revolution. He was one of the many who the communist revolution was supposed to save and lift out of poverty.

Tan from hard work in the sun and scrawny from walking up and down the highway to sell his fruit, one apple at a time, despite his age. The clothes he wore were worn, threadbare thin. He definitely looked like he lived only on fruit. I would even guess the fruit that he ate was probably the fruit which was too rotten to sell.

The outpour of the Cuban farmer continued. His grip on the car was fierce and his eyes were intense, probably even more so because he believed I was truly listening. I was. He wanted me to know. He wanted me to understand.

"El carne no entran en la carnecita!" (The meat does not come to the butcher shop.)

I was confused. Did he literally mean that there was no meat in the butcher shop or was he talking about the money and promises made by the Cuban government to its people. I did not know.

I was beginning to get the feeling that it was both.

There were tears in his eyes as he continued to speak. It was clear that he loved his country. He had lived a lifetime of hope for Cuba. For the advancement of Cuba. For the prosperity of Cuba. But it seemed he was met with many years of disappointment instead.

This man could have been my grandfather. He definitely was someone's grandfather. I imagined the stories he told his grandchildren, about the hopes and promises of the revolution. Maybe they had been too ambitious. Maybe they had miscalculated. Maybe the revolution hadn't been meant to save everyone. The farmer was a witness. He saw history everyday in his beloved Cuba, as he walked mile after mile to sell his fruit. He had waited for the promises. He had waited for the advancement. But as the years passed, disappointment replaced hope. The kind of disappointment that crushes the soul. He was sad. For his family, for his children, for his grandchildren.

And now, he was baring his heart. Not as a local does to a foreigner over a beer in a random bar. This was no ordinary declaration. No, this was different. This was a confession of a broken-hearted man for his country.

And I felt it. I keenly felt his pain. It made me immediately aware of what I had. My brand new car, the cash in my pocket (which was more than he would earn in a decade), my fortune of birth and circumstance.

While he was speaking, the song changed on the cd player. This drew my attention, from the man to the dashboard.

His eyes followed mine. Suddenly, he shook his finger and

raised his voice in declaration:

"No importa que me escuchen!" (I do not care who listens to me!)

Wow. He thought that my new car with my new radio and CD player - he thought it was a listening device, that the car was bugged. What life had this man lived to make this connection? That every CD player in Cuba was a listening device? How many other places and items were altered to listen into the conversations of their citizens?

Automatically, his outpour rose to a completely different level. Not only was he sharing his views, his heart, his disappointments, but he was doing so - or so he thought - at his own peril. He was acutely aware that freedom in Cuba did not include freedom of speech, nor did it include freedom from surveillance.

He continued on and spoke with great emotion of his love for Cuba, the Cuba that was, the Cuba that is, and the Cuba that he wanted it to be.

It could have been that this was a singular moment to share with someone, anyone, or maybe that it was rare to meet a foreigner. or maybe he didn't care. He didn't care who knew, who he told or what he told. The Cuban farmer was exhausted from it all. He wanted someone to know.

After a few minutes he came to a conclusion. He smiled at me while he slowly lifted his hands off the car. He had achieved an inner peace. And his eyes had became calm. They were no less intense but I could tell that he was content that someone had heard him.

He gestured for me to leave. As in an out-of-body experience, I turned the wheel and drove away.

In doing so, I felt different. From the connection. From the truths that I had heard. Even driving the car felt different, the music sounded different.

It amazed me how a short and seemingly innocent exchange of $20 for directions turned into a conversation which would alter the way I looked at the world. The way I looked at Cuba.

Disturbed by the insight into the complicated economic stature of Cuba, I decided not to contribute to it any longer, and shortly thereafter, I left.

I never forgot the man, his eyes, his tears, his passion, love, and disappointment in his country. I tell this story often not knowing if perhaps the fruit farmer was talking to me or in hopes of transmitting his despair, as an SOS to the world outside. In his mind, it might have been a way to change the future for his grandchildren. That perhaps his story, once told, would activate people to make a difference. The kind of difference he wanted and dreamt of, so many years ago at the beginning of the revolution.

And most of all, I remember his hope for Cuba and his love for his people. His words stay with me still. Each time I eat fruit, I remember him.

And thankfully, I eat fruit often.

———————————

Lagniappe

Call me cliché, but yes, you must drink Cuba Libre: rum and coke with splashes of lemon. You can have as many of these as you want while you make the national dish of Cuba: Ropa Vieja.

I could give you another dish which is better suited to the story but that is basically chopping up fruit and putting it in a bowl, otherwise known as fruit cocktail. You do not need me for that. For Ropa Vieja you kinda do.

Ropa Vieja

4 hours waiting. 15 minutes cooking. (It's worth it.)

2 pounds flank steak
2 tablespoons olive oil
1 cup beef broth
1 can tomato sauce
1 onion sliced
1 green bell pepper, chopped and seeded
2 garlic cloves, chopped
1 can tomato paste
1 teaspoon ground cumin
1 teaspoon fresh cilantro, chopped
1 tablespoon white vinegar

1. In heated skillet (medium high), brown the flank steak for 4 minutes on each side.

2. Transfer the beef to a slow cooker. Pour, dump, place all the rest into the cooker. Stir and blend. Cover. Sip your Cuba Libre. Wait for 4 hours.

3. When done, shred the meat and serve with rice or tortilla. Perhaps have some sour cream available on the side. And maybe another Cuba Libre. Or perhaps a cold beer. Or maybe a shot of tequila. Or water. As you like.

4. Serve fruit cocktail for dessert, of course.

"Walking with a friend
in the dark is better than
walking alone in the light."

Helen Keller

Burning Passports
Mexico

I am not sure, but I am thinking that maybe, just maybe, this might not be such a good idea.

I was trying to set pages of my passport on fire.

You see, we needed light. And I had already burned through all my money. Literally. Sadly, the flame only lasted a few seconds. No value there. What a waste of money. It wasn't spent on women, booze, or cars. I burned the cash for light.

You should know that I only came to that decision after trying to burn everything I was wearing: my socks, my shorts, my pants, my shirt.

This was no joke. Our survival depended on this.

So there I was: buck naked, sitting in the dark and about set fire to my passport.

We were lost inside this giant cave in Mexico. Caves are mazes made by nature. With death traps and no way out. There are no straight lines in a cave, no exit signs. More importantly, there is no water and no food.

And no light.

Which is all kind of crucial to survival. Yup, we were not in good shape. This was bad. This was really bad. I told myself not to panic but rather to focus on the solution.

Rip. Rip. Rip. Pages of the passport were being torn out. Rip some more.

I needed to be sure that we had enough to get us out, or at least to be able to see enough to put us on the right path.

We also needed to be perfectly ready for that last amount of gas in the lighter to catch. Because if it didn't...well, let's not focus on that right now.

The spark took. I held my breath. And prayed, prayed to every saint, God, my mother, and my father, that it would take.

One of them was listening. The pages of my passport took light. And it was glorious.

Exhale. Oh God, Thank you. Thank you.

Now that we could see, what next? Which direction should we take? We were in a cave which had several paths. If we chose the wrong one, we would be in even worse shape.

Lady luck, please? We flipped a coin and heads it was. We went left.

———

My nickname in school was Curious George. Not just because of my natural inquisitiveness but also because my penchant to climb everything. I love nature. Outdoor sports is my catnip. Add a little bit of risk and I am addicted. A lot of risk and you have my personal form of heroin.

What can I say? I am an adrenaline junkie.

This was different. I was working in New York and came down to Mexico for a small vacation. The customary tour seemed harmless but necessary, as the Mexican Park Rangers would not allow us into the cave alone. For reasons I was about to discover.

What happened? You see, there was a woman. (Isn't there always?) Actually, looking back, it was not really the woman. I was bored and there was this idiot trying to pick up this girl. Naturally, we started competing for her attention. And before long, there was a competition of "who is the coolest".

A competition like this is ok if only one of you is an adrenaline junkie. No harm done. But what happens when both of you are?

Well, we were about to find out.

————

Walking through the caves with the tour group, I was entranced. The stalagmites reaching the ceiling and stalactites coming down. I wanted to see if I could climb one. Who wouldn't? The entire place called, "Climb me."

Suddenly, I got this idea. Well, it was not really an idea because this was a competition, right? Or an excuse for me to climb. Or a hit of my personal form of heroin.

"Let's go check out this place," I said.
He smiled and replied, "Why not?"

"We will be right back," I said to the girl and disappeared around the corner with my current nemesis.

————

The caves were God's playground. Really. There is nothing like going where you should not be and testing your body to climb what you should not climb. Deeper and deeper into the caves we went. I was not worried about getting back because we both had flashlights.

That was until Simon fell. With only a small fracture, he was lucky. It could have been much worse, given the rock formations. The flashlight did not fare so well. That was gone. Simon brushed himself off, but it was clear we were not going to be running anywhere. The break was small, but nasty.

Our competition was over and we knew we had to get back. It could have been because of time, disorientation from the fall, or pure irresponsibility, but we could not find the group. They were gone. And the lights were off. The lights inside the cave that had turned on during our tour no longer were on.

More importantly, the exit that we expected to find was nowhere to be found. We were lost in the maze of a series of caves that went on for miles underground. If we took the wrong turn, we could very easily never see daylight again.

I started to feel the usual tingle of fear that warns me, a survival instinct. But, I told myself to stay cool. I was not panicking yet. I had the flashlight.

And then I ran out of battery.

Unbelievable. Curses erupted at each other, at ourselves. The flashlight received most of the abuse.

This was not helping anything. After blaming each other for a while, we agreed to be smart and settle down for the night. In the morning, we would wait for the tour to come back the next day, turn the lights on and find us. Right? We could not be so lost. Someone must be missing us, right?

Actually, the probability was high that no one was waiting for us. Except for the girl. Maybe. We both hoped that the girl would at least clock that we never returned before alerting authorities to start a search.

We could only hope. What we did know what that no one was coming now. Stifling our anxiety for the evening, we tried to get comfortable despite not being able to see anything. The blackness was blinding.

Despite it all, we both tried to keep the morale up, knowing that the sound of our voices would help reduce the panic. So, we talked. The combination of experiences of the day, the crash of the adrenaline of the day, fear of getting out, and pent up aggression lent to some great banter to keep the morale up, then some interesting conversations. And then the calm came, leading the way for a "bare soul" conversation.

There are conversations that one has with strangers at airports. There are conversations that one has with a priest. There are also conversations that one has when facing death. And then there are conversations you have when spending countless hours lost in the black dark cave.

We talked about everything. Family, girlfriends, the army, hopes, desires, fears and regrets. I learned Simon was about to go to Afghanistan. I won't share the details of what we talked about. It would seem cheap here. I told him things I had never told anybody and have not since. I gained a brother in the blackness that night.

The next day was interesting to say the least. A promise made the night before was that we were determined not to let the dark get to us, or to be petrified by the possibility of not getting out. We were never going to give up and we were going to get out.

First thing we did was to create a torch. We tried to burning our shirts, our shorts, our socks, and now we were going to burn our pants.

"Nothing like seeing a brother in his birthday suit," Simon commented.

I was really hoping that lighting the pants was going to be enough. Enough light to get us through this maze. A few trials, a few turns, it felt that we were even worse off than before.

This sucked. What next?

I thought of something. I actually had paper. In my pocket. It was cash. I thought if I ever was going to burn cash, it was not going to be in a cave with a naked man. It was going to be in a club with a naked woman but hey...beggars can't be choosers.

The most painful was the first bill. We didn't even move. We just watched it burn, in effigy. In reverence for the other bills that were about to be sacrificed.

Sadly, they were not worth their value in ash. And we were still lost.

Finally, we came to the conclusion that we should burn our passports. We flipped whose passport first would be to go: American or Canadian. A went before C.

I think Simon sang the "Star Spangled Banner" as we tried to light the way out. He was so sad that he had to burn his passport. God bless the Army boy.

Which was interesting, I did not feel the same way when I burned mine. Don't get me wrong, I am very proud of my country but at that moment, I didn't think of anything except that it had to get us out. National pride was not important.

Survival was.

———

With Simon limping, we could not run through the cave. I had to keep a slow enough pace to insure the light did not go out, but also so Simon could keep up.

Turning left was the right way to go, according to Lady Luck. By the time our passports had died to ash, we continued in silence, shuffling gently forward.

It felt like we crept for hours and hours. Not saying a word, barely holding our breath in hope.

And then finally, we heard voices.

Oh my Lord. Thank you. I have never been so happy to hear the voice of a police officer in my life.

The park rangers had a different attitude as did the police greeting us at the exit. Two foreigners climbing in their natural reservation and getting lost was not on top of their happy list. It was, however, top of their comedy list that we came out naked.

I didn't care. Light never looked so good.

We were given blankets and escorted to the police station where we waited. You can imagine the comments made by the people looking at us, the two naked climbers.

Simon did not speak Spanish, but I did, at least enough to ask for and get our first glass of water in days. Water will never taste the same. I still remember the taste.

Simon was taken to the hospital to get his leg tended to, and I had to stay behind to answer a multitude of questions. I was so tired and so relieved that I was not scared of the consequences, even if I had no idea what they were.

First, I had to register at the police station and when I was finished I was asked to wait. They probably wanted me to speak to an officer. Under other circumstances, I would be concerned but this time it was not a problem for me. I did not care. I was drinking water, standing in the sunshine coming from the window.

After an hour of waiting, I was called again to the desk to fill in more forms.

Stumbling forward in my blanket, I approached the desk.

"Tu passeporte, por favor," the officer asked, extending his hand waiting for me to give it to him.

Anything but that. The officer looked confused with my empty hands.

Smiling, I said: "Tengo un historia." I have a story to tell you.

"Lo quemé."

I burnt it.

Lagniappe

The drink of choice for this story is obviously water, given that our heroes went without it for days.

However, as far as food goes, the first meal that the starving boys may have had would be several plates of comfort food. First up would have been quesadillas, just to take the edge off. Easy, fast and so good.

Quesadilla
5 minutes

Large flour tortillas
Huge amounts of cheese: Monterrey Jack or cheddar
½ teaspoon olive oil for the pan
Add as much as you like:
Sliced mushrooms
Green onions, sliced
Olives, sliced
Tomatoes, diced
Chicken pieces, already grilled
Avocado

1. Add oil to hot pan, on medium heat, cover the base.

2. Add the tortilla, flip a few times at least 10 seconds between flips until small bubbles form.

3. Add the cheese and whatever your heart desires on top. Lower the heat and cover the pan.

4. Check to see when the cheese melts. When it has melted, take a spatula and flip one side of the tortilla on top, as if folding in half.

5. Flip again a few times to make sure it is browned. Done.

"The basic difference between an ordinary man and a warrior is that a warrior takes everything as a challenge while an ordinary man takes everything as a curse."

Don Juan

WRONG SIDE OF RAIN

West Africa

"Honey, are you ok?" I asked, as I dragged my girlfriend onto the river bank. Or was it she pulling me up. I did not know. I could not see through the sheets of water pouring down around us.

Outside of taking showers, swimming, or diving, I had never seen water like this. I was immersed. But I was not diving. I was standing on the side of a river bank, gasping for breath, drenched from the rain. That's right. Rain. The kind of rain where there is more water in the sky than in the sea.

For me, it was a rain of epic proportions. For the villagers we had just left, it was just another rainy day in Africa. They were used to this.

I, however, was not. I was not really used to driving down roads in the morning, and then returning in the afternoon to see that very road had become a river. Nope. That was not my kind of normal.

My kind of normal was 'leisurely drive in the safari,' not 'sitting in a car which was learning to swim.' And definitely not the kind where 'flooding the engine' actually meant a 'flood in the engine'.

Literally.

Water was coming in through the windows. From the sky. And also from below. What was once a dirt road with a few puddles and potholes was now white water rapids.

Yup. Another day in Africa. This was Adventure 101. How to make a Land Cruiser swim.

But before that, we needed a plan to get out of the car and onto 'dry land'. I would prefer to enact any plan in the next minute or so. Because with the water having already reached our waistline, it was borderline urgent.

Everyday is a learning opportunity. At least, now I know how Noah felt.

The day started as most Saturdays did: a good breakfast, chill out around the home in the morning before my girlfriend and I head out to go exploring. We lived in West Africa, and for us, any day and every hour is a good time to go exploring.

After picking up my friend Chris, we decided that this weekend we would not follow any map and just drive with the intention to get lost, and see where the road would take us. We were going to drive west, off the highway and into the bush. Who can fault us that? This is the way most discoveries are made, no?

After several hours in the car, down rugged terrain, dirt roads, and under a blistering sun, we came across a few huts. Mud huts to be exact.

It seemed to be deserted. But as soon as we got out of the car, we could hear people sing and shout. It sounded like a party. Their voices drew us towards one of the mud huts and we peeked inside. The entire village was inside. There must have been at least 60 people laughing, singing, and dancing.

And then they saw us. And immediately everyone went silent. After a few seconds of tension, a shout of welcome came from the crowd. Which was then echoed throughout the group. Their surprise turned to smiles. Open arms greeted us. Drunk and happy, they offered what they had, charcoaled corn on the cob and their corn moonshine. I am always touched by the amazing generosity of those who have nothing, and yet they offer everything. We tried to say, "No, thank you" (not wanting to take what little they had), but they would not have it.

Honored by their kindness, we humbly accepted and happily joined in the celebration. (I need to tell you now that my dancing is absolutely fantastic after several gulps of corn moonshine. And my breakdancing is world class.)

After several hours with our new found friends, it was time to leave. The skies were turning dark - never a good sign. We did not want to get lost in the bush after nightfall.

The word "nightfall" describes exactly what happens in Africa: the night falls on you like a blanket. There is no light. And it happens quickly, before you know it: boom. And then total darkness.

Total darkness in the bush. Not the best place to be. Already, the skies were dark. And, moreover, there was an audible quiet, as if every single animal had gone for cover. Like the jungle had a code, a warning that something was about to happen.

It was the silence before a storm.

Rain fell. And fell. And fell some more. I remember thinking there is so much rain, swimming in my clothes would have the same effect.

Little did I know, that was exactly what was going to happen.

Note to self: never challenge Mother Earth.

Of course, when you plan on getting lost on purpose, you probably are going to get lost on the way back. It's a guess. The breadcrumbs we had left on the way were now gone, washed away.

As was the road we had been on. After a few hours, we finally made it back to the main road. We could see it ahead and exhaled with the recognition of a familiar landmark. This meant we were halfway home.

And then we got closer. What was once a road was now a river.

I am not joking, people. When I say, rain. It rains. It was not a shimmering drizzle. Not a spring shower. Nope. The road was now a river, with enormous swells of muddy brown water.

The way that the water was coming, the only choice was to go forward. We could not go back.

And so into the river, we drove. Fish gotta swim right?

We are not fish. I have never been a fish. Nor has my car been a fish. But that was what we were attempting to do: make our car swim.

As if we could float above the mud and the potholes. You know, when you have one crazy idea to drive your car into a river, don't stop there. Let more crazy ideas come. Like keep on doing the same thing, especially when you get stuck. The tires were now spinning in water, the trunk was gargling and the hood was gurgling.

All 'good' signs. Including the river coming into your back seat.

The crazy ideas we had a few minutes before were now being replaced with reality, accompanied by a small dose of panic. We were stranded in the middle of nowhere, with water rising ever higher around the car, already level with the windows. (Did I mention that we had not told anyone where we were going that morning? Of course not. That would be crazy. Responsibility? I laugh in your face. I am not sure which was louder: the slapping of self or the expletives to accompany the gesture.)

Chris took the initiative, pointing to the left of the car where there was a plot of land not yet touched by the rapids.

"You guys get out and I will try and drive."

It sounded like a plan. At least someone had a plan. And right now that plan was to get out of the car through the sunroof and swim. As we climbed out, Chris started revving the engine. It worked. Amazing, right? Yes, God bless Land Cruiser. It must have been built for water as well as rugged terrain. He let go of the throttle, powering the car up and out of the hole it had fallen into. The engine whined at the strain. We could hear the car gurgle while the wheels were spinning in the muck under water.

It looks kind of like the splash you make when you swim free-style. But different.

The car started moving agonizingly slowly. I think by this time we were praying. And lo and behold, Chris drove the car up and and onto 'firmer muck' before turning the car back into the river, with huge waves of brown water splashing up and over them. We had faith in Chris that he knew how to navigate through the water, the great mariner he is.

Chris was aiming for the newly formed river bank on the other side. For a moment that stretched into eternity, we watched in horror as the car was stuck on the edge of the bank, slipping back and forth between the relative safety of the track and the dark waters beneath it.

Until finally, with a sigh of relief, Chris managed to get the car onto dry land.

We whooped. We jumped. We hugged. We felt like we had won.

But wait a second. Don't pull out that moonshine too fast.

The car was on land. And that land was on the other side of the river.

The other side.

Of the river.

Of course.

————

"Well," I thought. "If the car can swim, then so can I."

And into the raging brown rapids we went. Not easy for anyone. To be 'carried away' is fine if you read the word in a romantic novel. Not so much in real life, when you are fighting for survival in whitewater rapids, in the middle of nowhere. My panic was now replaced with adrenaline. (What am I saying? The adrenaline was always there.)

Seriously, where is Moses when you need him?

(You know, the benefits to torrential rain is that you don't really need a water bottle to rinse your mouth when you swallow mud by accident. It is kind of a open and spit deal. Silver lining, gotta find them.)

We waded carefully through the muddy sludge with the current tugging at our legs and feet. We had to be careful not to lose our footing, since it was safer to wade than to swim against the current. We sloshed to and fro in order to find the shallowest parts around us, until we eventually managed to make it to the other side.

Safe. And ok.

We all were.

Thank you, Poseidon.

————

We punched the air in victory. After crossing the "Red Sea", I went to our car and hugged it.

"Thank you. Now, please, please, do not let us down, you fabulous piece of machinery and take us home."

I was really hoping our car had come out intact from this ordeal. Because if it broke down, we would be in even bigger trouble than before. Why? Night was about to fall, the great blanket of darkness.

(You know what, kids? When you leave home, tell your parents. Try not to do as I do and end up in the middle of the bush in a broken down car. It is just not cool.)

We did not break down. The car gods were with us. Land Cruisers rock. There were a few more times when we held our breath, including several minutes when I do not think I even inhaled. It was while we drove up this particularly steep slope. A few hours earlier this would not have been a problem, but after the flooding rain, it was now going to be a challenge. Especially with a deep ravine on one side of the car. I could not see the bottom from my window.

Did I mention panic? Or adrenaline? Where was the moonshine when I needed fortification?

Thankfully (and most likely due to Chris's skill and expertise at driving a 4x4), we managed to avoid the fate of tumbling darkness and muck ridden roads, including whatever creatures were waiting for their 'dinner'.

The moment we saw the gates of our home, we broke out in laughter and shouts of victory. We were celebrating arriving at home and in our voices you could probably hear some relieved hysteria along with overwhelming amounts of testosterone. Safe on the other side, we were now reveling in the amazing experience we had just lived: the panic, the adrenaline, the corn, the dancing, the huts, the tribe, the moonshine, the swim. And the river.

"Let's do it again!" I am not sure if it was just me who said it out loud or if we all did in unison.

I kid you not. This is exactly what we did the following Saturday.

However, this time I was prepared. This time I told my friends where we were going. And, this time I brought my swimming trunks with me.

But don't worry, I was not leaving home without the Land Cruiser.

You see, I was on a mission.

I wanted the recipe for that corn moonshine.

Lagniappe

Plantains and yams are everywhere in West Africa. Chop the plantain into triangles, deep fry them, dry on paper towel, salt and serve. Easy.

Of course, frying plantains is not really a recipe. I thought you might like this one: Jollof Rice which is found on every West African table. Every. Single. One. And rightly so.

What to drink with jollof rice? Moonshine, of course! However, in case you do not have your own private still, try a cold beverage of choice: beer or wine. Last time I made this dish, I served it together with a chilled pinot noir. (I don't have a private still either.)

Jollof Rice
50 minutes

1 cup chicken breast
1 tablespoon ground paprika
2 tablespoons cayenne
1 onion, sliced
1 celery, sliced
1 green pepper, sliced and seeded
3 garlic cloves
½ inch piece ginger
1 carrot, cubed
3 tablespoons tomato paste
2 large tomatoes, chopped
¼ cup olive oil

½ tablespoon butter
1 teaspoon dried thyme
¼ teaspoon curry powder
1 bay leaf
½ cup mushroom
½ cup peas
2 cups rice (Not instant)
2 cups chicken stock
2 cups water
1 chicken stock cube

Season with salt and pepper. Garnish with cilantro.

Put butter and oil in a large pot and saute: chicken breast, paprika, cayenne, onion, celery, green pepper, garlic, and ginger, for 3 - 4 minutes.

Add carrots.

Add tomato paste, tomatoes, and everything else except for the rice and liquids. Cook until you see the oil and butter in the pan start to turn red and the tomatoes turn soft.

Add the rice and saute for 2 to 3 minutes.

Add the rest of the water, chicken stock, chicken stock cube and then close the lid and wait for the rice to cook through until soft.

If the water has evaporated and the rice is still hard, add a half cup of water and check again in 5 minutes to make sure that the rice does not turn to mush.

That's it! Enjoy!

"Toto, I've got a feeling we are not in Kansas anymore."

Dorothy in The Wizard of Oz

LET'S DO LUNCH
Kenya & Zanzibar

"So you feel like it? Lunch?" he asked.

"Sure. Why not? Where are you thinking?" A lunch date would be lovely. If he wanted to, we could eat at the canteen close to where I worked. Harmless, right? Not that I was opposed to 'harm', looking at him. This guy was straight up delicious. What can I say? I blame the African heat. I was getting hot.

Joking aside, I was way overdue for a good time. I had been working non-stop since my arrival in Kenya. It was back-breaking work as a water engineer in an under-staffed humanitarian NGO. I had not been out at all. So, I thought a lunch date with Mr. Sexy here was definitely on my menu. Even if it was salad at the local canteen.

"Great," he said. "I'll pick you up here tomorrow." He smiled and my heart flipped. It actually flipped. Suddenly, I had a feeling, an intuition, that I could be in trouble here. That perhaps I was not the 'hunter' in this dating game. Because with those eyes and that smile came with dimples. Let's just call the entire package: trouble.

Thank god it was only lunch. I followed a 5 date rule at home. But, honestly, do you think it applies when you are working in Africa? I mean I was living in the land of the birds, the bees, and the zebras, and the hippos. Surely, sexual morality is different here, right?

I was getting ahead of myself. He had only asked me for lunch. Perfectly respectable. I told myself to put away the red light.

Walking away, he turned and yelled, "Bring your passport!"

"What? Wait. What? Where are we going? Why do I need my passport?" Questions abound. We are literally in the middle of nowhere. Uhm, and besides, I have a job. What happened to the canteen? Isn't that romantic enough? I was too stunned by his request to ask for details. And given my stupefaction complete with dropped jaw, the opportunity left with him as he drove away.

But when he pulled up the next day, I was ready. My jaw was back in place and I had my passport in hand. After kissing me on the cheek hello, we made a quick exit and started driving down the dirt road away from the NGO, passing the canteen in a cloud of dust. I assumed that the necessity of my passport eliminated the notion of lunch at said canteen; ergo, I only knew where we were not going.

After driving for about 20 minutes, we passed a sign that gave directions to the airport. Smiling, I grabbed his shoulder and shook it.

"Where are we going?" I asked. "Aren't you going to tell me?"
"I am taking you to lunch," he winked.

He winked. The man with dimples made by the devil: winked. I was definitely in trouble.

Five minutes later, we pulled up to a small twin engine two seater plane. I looked at him in shock. Where did this plane come from? Where did this airport come from? Because this was not an airport. This was a landing strip. Actually, this was not a landing strip; this was a dirt road with zebras grazing on it.

And where was the pilot? I did not see any pilot. I saw giraffes. I saw zebras. But no pilot. Nope. No uniform. No captain.

No

one.

Looking at him, with questioning eyes and raised eyebrows, I asked, "Who exactly is flying?"

Mr. Devil Dimples winked again.

"I am," he replied.

Of course he was.

He walked to the plane, holding his hand out to follow him.

"Ready?" he asked.

"Born ready," I replied.

You know, looking back, I never asked him for his pilot's license.

Less than 10 minutes later, we were in the air. Of course, the dimpled devil knew how to fly. Of course he did. How silly of me. Normal humans drive cars but not here. The risk and 'cool' factor of riding motorbikes was so probably so 'yesterday'. Testing my theory, I wondered if he had one.

I spoke into the headset, "Do you have a motorbike?"

He looked at me, as if I had asked him if he could spell.

"Sure, I have a few at home. Why? Do you ride?"

Of course he did. And of course I don't. I am from a small town with two overprotective parents. If I wanted speed on two wheels, I needed to peddle faster.

"What do you feel like?" he continued nonchalantly. As if we were at the canteen, our local pizza parlor, choosing between whether we should have extra pepperoni or vegetarian topping.

But we were not choosing between pizza toppings. And we were definitely not in Kansas anymore. I think the view from above gave it away: the pink flamingos, stirred by the sound to the plane, began to take flight. We skirted the trees, circled by giraffes. I look down as the gazelles and zebras looked up before starting to race the plane's shadow on the open fields of the safari.

"I know this great place," he said into the headset, "It's on the beach."

"Where?" I asked.

"Zanzibar."

Of course.

———————

If he wanted to impress me, he was succeeding. I felt like Karen Blixen flying over miles and miles of Safari. After a while, we met the ocean, and started flying over the waves. It looked like rippling silk curtains of sapphire blue.

Before I knew it, we saw an island in the distance. And the beach came closer and closer. Looking down, I saw the water change from sapphire to emerald. And as we got closer to shore, I could see all the way to the bottom, even from the plane. I wanted to jump out and dive into its precious depths.

"I did not bring a bikini," I murmured to myself.

I think he heard me. Mr. Dimples smiled.

Maybe that was the point.

We landed a little north of Stone Town, touching down on a small runway, coming to a full stop on the field near a lone building built like a cement brick. It was stone grey and had huge white billboards with the crest of Zanzibar emblazoned on them. The landing strip was also scattered with military jeeps and a few old Mercedes, rusting soft in the African sun.

Three soldiers in a Jeep drove towards us. One was standing up in the back seat, yelling at us, while two soldiers sat in front, serene in their power. I had a fleeting moment of concern before Mr. Dimples squeezed my hand.

"Don't worry. I know these guys."

Of course you do.

And of course he did.

I do not know why I even bought my passport. It was a breeze.

The three soldiers hardly even looked at my passport before ushering us into their car and driving to the building.

When we got inside, Mr. Devil Wears Dimples was speaking Swahili to them all. Of course he spoke fluent Swahili. He high-fived every soldier and customs officer, calling them each by name, giving them each the "African handshake".

What gauntlet of protection? This was a homecoming. He was king here.

I was beginning to think that he had done this before.

As we were walking towards the door, back into the sunlight, one of the soldiers threw him a pair of car keys. He caught them mid-air, not even breaking stride.

He had definitely done this before.

He opened the door for me before getting in himself. I double checked. Wasn't this the same jeep as the customs officers? I guess, if he didn't mind, neither would I.

Smiling at me, he put on his sunglasses while turning the key to the engine.

"You are going to love this place. Everything is fresh. Fresh from the sea."

I think I was learning to roll with it. Of course it was fresh. Of course it was from the sea. And of course we had just waltzed through customs, and of course we were using their car to eat fresh fish. In Zanzibar.

Oh brother. I was in trouble. He definitely knew how to treat a girl.

We drove to the north of the island, to what I imagine must have been the exact same beach he had pointed out crossing over in the plane.

The main road was lined with vendors of every kind and locals making their daily living. We stopped for a bottle of water before continuing on to a small rocky road until it came to a dead end. We were facing a gate which was made of flowers, intense in floral drapery and color: blood red orange and fluorescent fuchsia intermingled with vines of deep green.

Underneath one of the trees sat a small boy who immediately upon sight, started waving to us. With an excited greeting, he ran to open the gates.

We drove through and parked under a hanging canopy of lush green leaves. I exited the car and took it all in. It seemed as if I had stepped into the Garden of Eden. Nature's foliage was so intense. Smiling, Mr. Dimples took my hand, guiding me through the trees and led me to a patio with sofas and tables. It was part of a two-sided house. As we climbed the steps to the patio, I could see straight through to the ocean, the white beaches and emerald waters. The house only added to the experience, acting as a live picture frame to the incredible sight before us.

The patio was empty of people as we passed through towards the beach. The beauty beckoned me. I wanted to get my feet wet. I wanted to go in. This was incredible. So amazingly beautiful. The emerald sea called to me, an invitation complete with a pathway lined with white satin sand.

Shaking off my shoes, I walked towards the water barefoot. My toes curled in the sensation of the warm sand. I raised my hands and saluted the sun. It was amazing to be here.

Taking in the panoramic view, I saw a small shack to the left. It was made of drift wood, protecting a makeshift barbecue pit from the wind and rain. Underneath stood three oil drums, sawed in half. Supported by bricks, they were belly down, full of coal and working as a barbecue pit, guarded by an elderly man with bright eyes and an even brighter smile.

He called us over. He must have been another long lost brother. We were welcomed with hugs and invited to sit at their prime spot. I looked at the plastic table and chairs situated on the edge of the water, ebbing and flowing. It is difficult to describe the sensation of sitting down, eating a glorious meal, while the crystal warm waters of the Indian Ocean playing with our feet.

It was surreal. (As a water engineer, I was used to working with different water, dark and dirty. This made the transportation to this paradise all the more potent.)

Before long, we were served. The fish was fresh. Of course. It had been taken off the pit and served on plastic plates, together with a pot of honey. Strange, I thought. Honey and fish? Really? He took the pot and drenched the fish in the honey. Drenched it. The fish could have swum in the honey, if it hadn't been already grilled to perfection.

Of course it was delicious.

And of course, he fed me.

With sticky fingers, my hands were up. I surrender. This was more than any girl could ever imagine. That I could ever conceive of. In my lifetime.

Covered with honey from the meal, we were sticky. And hot. And a bit dusty. The water had been inviting us for hours.

There was really only one thing to do...

Swim.

With no swimsuit.

Besides...

Who needs a bikini when you have a passport?

Lagniappe

This is probably the easiest and sexiest dish of all. Hands down. Definitely a memory making dish. Have cold beer or chilled white wine. Any smooth cool drink that refreshes you while you play.

Floating In Honey Fish
20 minutes

2 flounder steaks
1 jar honey
Lemon or orange wedges

1. Clean the fresh flounder.
2. Cut 3 slashes into it.
3. Place in aluminum foil.
4. Pour honey all over it.
5. Until it drowns.
6. Fold the aluminum over the fish, like a pocket.
7. Puncture hole into pocket to allow for smoke.
8. Place on grill, medium heat.
9. 10 minutes per inch of thickness.
10. Serve with orange or lemon wedges.
11. Lick each other's fingers.

"Don't count the days.
Make the days count."

Muhammed Ali

OUR TSUNAMI BABY
Thailand

PART I

We did not know what the word "tsunami" meant before that day.
No one did.
Now, we know.

————

This unfathomable tragedy began on Boxing Day morning in Banda Aceh, a small Indonesian town on the island of Sumatra. It was the first landfall to be hit by the tsunami, caused by a massive (magnitude 9.3) earthquake under the Indian Ocean.

It remains as one of the deadliest natural disasters in history, killing an est. 280,000 people in 14 countries, inundating coastal communities with waves up to 30 metres/100 feet high.

But what does this really mean? In an age of war, we are so used to hearing news of deaths. We become numb to the numbers, forgetting that real people are the "statistic".

So before recounting Mark and Sally's story, I wanted to create some color with 3 facts, since I believe a Google search would not do it justice.

1) The tsunami came from the third largest earthquake ever recorded. The last time a tsunami of this magnitude happened was during the Roman Empire.

It caused the entire planet to move 1 centimeter on its axis.
1 centimeter.
Not even the power of the Sun does that.

To give another example, the force created by the earthquake and the resulting tsunami was more than the energy of the combination of all the bombs dropped during World War II. In fact, it was registered to be more than 15,000 x more powerful than the atomic bomb dropped on Hiroshima.

It was this force that created waves 10 stories high, laying waste to 14 countries. It was not a flood. Floods do not move through houses and break them apart like toothpicks.

But a 'flood' with the force of 15,000 nuclear bombs can.

2) Children, happy with their presents from the day before (Christmas), were up early, frolicking on the beach, playing in the warm waters. They were fascinated by all the fish left on the sand.

A beach had been created that morning. As a result of the earthquake, a tsunami formed by pulling water from everywhere, creating massive waves 10 stories high.

Less than a half an hour of the water pulling away, it returned.
In a completely different form.

More than half of the 280,000 people that died that morning were children. They drowned instantly and were carried out to sea with the exiting current.

Never to be found. Never to be buried.

3) On the morning after Christmas 2004, the town of Banda Aceh had a population of 7,500. By evening, it was 400. Everything was gone. Everything.

More than 14 countries were devastated that day. The last time Sweden lost that many citizens was in 1709, at the Battle of Poltava.

While celebrating Christmas, families of all nations were torn apart, in every horrific way imaginable. The engulfing waves separating them, permanently.

Without warning. Without a last "I love you", they were gone, leaving those who survived to live the nightmare.

Not many people knew what a tsunami was before December 26, 2004. Now, we all do. For the survivors, Boxing Day will be an anniversary of devastation. And for many a memorial of loss and death.

But not for these this couple.

————

"Wow, a tremor," I thought to myself, wondering what it was. The bed shook a little and the curtains moved. I looked at my water glass on the bedside table. The water was moving.

I leaned over and patted my wife awake, "Did you feel that?"

My wife mumbled, "no", before turning back to sleep. I shrugged my shoulders, peacefully ignorant with no idea of what had just happened.

What that "small tremor" actually was.

————

I got up. I knew something was wrong. Ignoring the uneasy feeling in my stomach, my wife and I went downstairs for breakfast. Entering the restaurant, smiles greeted us everywhere. The Thai people are always so happy.

And why shouldn't they? They live in paradise. Today we were all smiling. It was still Christmas. My favorite time of the year. Normally, we would be in England; I must admit I missed my family and the yuletide traditions. But then I pinched myself as I looked out over the beautiful view of the beach. We were spending Christmas in paradise.

As we sat down to eat, we noticed a surge of water entering the lagoon. This seemed a little odd to us. I mean, we knew something was not quite right, probably because we had no idea what "wrong" actually looked like. Despite feeling unsettled, we continued with our Boxing Day brunch.

And then, we heard a single scream.
Immediately followed by more screams.
Then everyone was screaming.

In a split second the calm turned to fear. The serenity to panic. And the quiet became an avalanche of screams. What had just happened?

I saw terror on everyone's faces.

A tsunami had hit Thailand. Our very shores.

The news had come of a tidal wave, an avalanche of water that submerged the coast of Thailand, and drowned all that came into contact with it: all the tourists that were in Thailand to celebrate Christmas, all families and homes of the people that worked at the resort. The news was that their very existence was now underwater. The horror of what had just happened and the devastating effect did not immediately register. Slowly, we realized it was not just a tsunami of water, it was a tsunami of tragedy, devouring everything its path; leaving destruction, loss, sorrow, and death.

By some "fluke of nature", our hotel had avoided being hit. The natural lagoon had shielded us. Our hotel was quickly transformed into a refuge center.

Locals and guests at the neighbouring hotels were not so lucky. If they had survived the tsunami, if they had found all their family members, by the time they reached the hotel/shelter; they were battered and torn. Their lives destroyed.

The following hours felt surreal with the mix of emotions: shock at the news reports and local accounts of the damage, grief over the loss of lives, disbelief that this had really happened, and relief that we were unscathed.

The question "what if" was constant in all of our minds.
What if we had chosen to stay at another hotel?
What if we had not slept in and taken a walk on the beach that

morning?

What if we had died?

With no chance to do what I want to do?

Live the life I want to live, a family life?

All those questions would be answered later. Right now our focus was on everyone else. Not us. We were not deserving. We had survived. Instead, we tried to help the locals as much as we could in the search for their missing family members. And the guests searching for their loved ones who might have been lost in the waves.

Furthermore, the telephone lines were down. We were isolated. And so was the rest of the world, handicapped with distance, trying to get through in order to hear the good news, proof of life.

Those hours, those days, are indescribable. Living with the nightmare, we tried to comfort as many as possible, to help those who were less fortunate. It all passed by in a blur of tears, devastation, hope, and tragedy.

———

A few days later, on the way to the airport, we drove through a nearby town of Patong, seeing first hand the debris and destruction left by the wave. We could see where it had stopped: on one side, there was complete devastation, and on the other it looked as if nothing had happened. We passed by a house where a huge dumper truck was wedged into the side of the second floor. I thought to myself, "My God. If a wave can lift a truck that weighs several tons, imagine how vulnerable the people were?"

Quiet in our thoughts, we spent the rest of the drive fighting the waves of panic after having witnessed more signs of death.

What we saw at the airport has become one of the most harrowing experiences of our lives, deep empathy for our fellow human beings and the tragedy they were experiencing. Their heart ache. Their despair.

The departure hall had become a missing persons center, where loved ones manned sections of the area where they paced, searching and praying that they would find their family members. Clasping to the last straws of hope that they could have survived.

The walls were covered with posters of adults and children. Hundreds of pictures were stuck on the wall. Each one placed there in desperate hope that someone would recognise a face and bring about a miracle, a survival.

But there were only tears, only red eyes, only despair. People were sitting on the floor in obvious shock. Numb. Catatonic.

The grief was palpable and something we will never, ever forget.

I had heard of survivor's' guilt before, but had not understood it. Until now. How were we so lucky to have escaped death and destruction?

We looked at the pictures on the wall and then we looked at each other. We had each other. We had survived.

PART II

Later that evening we arrived home, safe and sound in Singapore. Although it was New Year's Eve, frivolities and festivities were ignored. Instead, we embraced the opportunity to stay in, enjoy a glass of wine and begin the journey of digesting the last few days.

The questions of "what if" had never left our minds. We were well aware that our survival was a "gift", an opportunity to act. We decided then and there that this event must make a positive influence on our lives.

We decided to adopt a tsunami baby, a child that had lost its parents as a result of the tragedy.

Making that decision, we felt as if all the puzzle pieces had come together. We both felt it was right. Moreover, it was something we could not wait to be:

Parents.

———

As British expats living in Singapore, we were governed by strict, but relatively speedy adoption laws. Thankfully, there were many specialist agencies to help couples navigate the bureaucracy, while protecting the young children.

In our first interview, we learned that our chances of adopting a "tsunami baby" would be slim. A wall had been built to protect these young lives from the vultures who profit by baby trafficking. The other reality was that very few babies had survived the tsunami without their parents.

The children had perished first, being far more vulnerable to the power of the wave. The survivors were picked up by baby traffickers.

Horrific.

We were not deterred. We continued our search. We wanted to adopt.

We looked outside of Thailand. And turned to Indonesia.

It seemed to be the right choice, given the huge loss of life that country had suffered. The wheels were put in motion for the agency to find a baby girl. While they looked, we began the extensive vetting process.

———

Our decision on the 1st of January became a reality later in April. Our agent called with the news that a three week old baby girl had been handed in to a "halfway house"; her parents could not afford to raise her.

"Would you like to meet her?" she asked.

"Would we like to meet her? Are you kidding?"

On Sunday, the 4th of April 2005, we took a boat to the island of Batam, Indonesia. The ride took less than an hour but it seemed like a few seconds. We could hardly wait to meet our baby girl.

It remains one of the most special days in our lives. Our memories are vivid: the clothes we wore, the scarf we bought to shield against the wind, the smell of the water, the boat ride, the anticipation of our future with our baby. Our new family.

As we entered the "halfway house", our agent told us about bonding with the child, and that we were under no obligation to adopt the baby if we felt no "connection". I knew what she meant, clearly recalling the connection with my son at the moment of his birth, 12 years ago. It felt like a lightning bolt of love and protection.

My guess is that the agent was preparing us, having lived through many unsuccessful adoptions in the past. But with us, she had nothing to fear.

Not remotely.

When a little baby girl, wrapped in a tea towel, was bought out, my wife cried, "Darling, this is Mali!"

We knew our daughter immediately. The connection of instant love, of being a mother, of being a father, for both of us, was instantaneous. It was love at first sight.

Looking at her, we knew that the name we had chosen for her was perfect. In Thai, "Mali" not only means "jasmine" but also "flowering beauty". And that she was.

Our little beauty was tiny, sleepy and beautiful.
We could not stop looking at her.
We had found our daughter.
We had found our family.

———

Our agent happily started the next steps in our adoption. According to the law in Singapore, first precautions had to be taken to ensure that our little girl was not a carrier of the HIV virus. We brought a pediatrician with us to Bantam so that the tests could be carried out immediately.

I held one of Mali's hands as the pediatrician drew blood from the other. Feeling the prick of the needle, Mali let out a tiny cry.

I moved my face next to hers, whispering, "It's okay Mali, Daddy is here!" Her eyes moved towards my voice and she stopped.

And smiled.

My daughter smiled at me.

———

We had to leave her in Batam that day to wait the agonizing 24 hours for the HIV test results. We would get the news directly from the hospital in Singapore, which is where we decided to wait. Drinking coffee, we talked about what would we do if our little princess was HIV positive. It was not even a question. She was our daughter. Nothing was going to stand in our way of being her parents. No matter what.

When we got the news that Mali's blood results were normal, we started jumping up and down. Coffee splattered all over the hospital floor but we didn't care. We were euphoric. It was only a matter of days before Mali could come home.

———

While the papers were being filed, we visited Mali the following weekend. In that short period of one week, the medications and food we had left for her began to take effect. Our little girl had transformed from a mosquito bitten, "scrap of a thing" into a true "flowering beauty".

She was more splendid than we had remembered.
In her new clothes, she was adorable.

We spent every possible moment with Mali before she was allowed to travel to Singapore to start her new life. On Friday, the 22nd of April 2005, Mali came home. At the hospital, the doctor handed her over to us, delivering her to us. There were tears of joy, laughter and happiness. We were so lucky to be parents to this beautiful little girl.

Back at our apartment, we were overwhelmed with emotion as we placed Mali in her little baby chair and watched her sleep.

The tsunami of tragedy had turned into a tsunami of happiness as we looked at each other and our little girl. Our family. Home.

This is not the end of the story. In August of that year, we returned to the resort in Phuket, to renew our wedding vows, with Mali and my son, Luke, by our side.

We needed to be at the island and the hotel to celebrate what the tsunami had given us: Mali.

Today, as I write our story, Mali is exactly one month short of her 12th birthday. I look across the table as she studies for school in Spain. She is and has always been a gift to us. A gift of life.

Each time I look at her, a different tsunami overwhelms me.

One of love.

Lagniappe

This story inspires me to drink champagne. How can you not? If any drink is renown for celebrating life, love, and family: it is champagne. So, raise your glass and salute those you love.

Afterwards, if you get hungry, here is classic, easy to make, hands-down, great Thai recipe. Tom Yung Goong soup. It is a classic for good reason: cheap, fast, and oh-so-delicious. And spiceeeee. Just the way I like it.

Now you can pair champagne with this dish (in my opinion, bubbles go with everything), but if you want to simulate how I would eat this in Thailand, it would always be with a Singha beer.

Tom Yung Goong Soup

20 minutes

1 cup shrimp
4 cups water
3 chili peppers
5 sprigs cilantro
2 tablespoons fish sauce
3 kaffir lime leaves
1 lemongrass
2 limes
5 mushrooms
1 tablespoon Nam Prig Pow (if you can find it)

1. While boiling the water, pound the lemongrass a bit to release the flavor before placing it in the pot of water.

2. After cleaning the shrimp, prepare the bowls by putting the fish paste, chili pepper, and lime juice on the bottom of the bowl.

3. Add the mushrooms, lime leaves and the shrimp to the boiling water. As soon as the shrimp change color, they are done.

4. Scoop out the soup and place in the bowl. Add the nam prig pow, if you can, and top with cilantro.

Have fun. Delicious. Easy. And hot. It's yum yum soup.

"Every once in a while, Whiskey Tangoes the Foxtrot...Good thing I know how to drink and dance."

Unknown

White Gloves in the Jungle

Congo

I lifted up my hand and closed it into a fist, signaling to my platoon behind me that they should stop. The silence became quieter. I held my breath.

For days, we had been marching through the heat, humidity, and dense vegetation of the Congolese jungle. Even though I could not see 5 meters in front of me. I suddenly sensed humans ahead.

Making a split second decision with my signal, we started forward, primed and ready in tactical formation. We were on a reconnaissance mission. And according to my briefing and map, there were no villages here.

There should be no one in this part of the Congo.

No one.

————

Quietly pushing aside the brush, I saw a mirage appear before me, glimmering through a haze of mist. I wiped my eyes to make sure of what I saw.

For this was not real.

There was no way this could be real. This was definitely not what I expected. What any of us had expected.

"Welcome, sir. We have been waiting for you," I heard a voice say.

I looked around. It was a butler. And not just one butler, but a battalion of them, tall and proud wearing uniforms of white ties and tail coats. I walked towards them and was stopped by another flank of butlers, also in white tie and tails.

They were holding silver trays of crystal flutes of champagne. In surreal slow motion, they offered them to us. All of them simultaneously raising their trays, choreographed with a stiff bow.

As if in a dream, my hand reached for a glass and was struck by what I saw, questioning reality. There was the elegance and refinement of the flutes, the champagne, and the white gloves holding the silver platter. And then the stark contrast to my hand: dark with filth, scratched, and bloody.

I was not on my way to a ball. I was nowhere near home. I was not even in the same continent as home. I was in the jungle.

Where I had been parachuted in 5 days before.

And since then, we had been living in the elements, sleeping in the rain, trudging through mud, forging through the intense vegetation and incredible humidity. My platoon and I had slept on the ground. In the same clothes. In the mud. In fact, we were covered in it. And the entire time, we had not seen a single house.

Until now.
But this was no house.
This was no mirage.
This was a plantation.
In the jungle.
In the Congo.
In the middle of nowhere.

Candles lit the path of polished pebble stones, leading up to the front door of the pillared mansion, white and resplendent in its majesty, glimmering in the moonlight. Large French doors allowed for easy access to the wide porch wrapping around the entire home. The windows were open, lending light to the outside garden. I could hear the lilting music as it escaped from the house into the thick night air where it battled with a concert of crickets.

Where butlers in white tie were meeting us, offering champagne.

I could not be hallucinating this. I turned to my platoon, my mates, my soldiers in arms. Each of them had dropped his jaw in disbelief. Their reaction confirmed our reality. We had not been made aware of this place. Which we should have, given that we were on reconnaissance mission.

How did all this get here? Where did it all come from? I wondered. The only way to get here was the same way we came. Out of the sky. With parachutes.

We were led up the candle lit walkway into the mansion. Holding onto our champagne flutes with our gritty hands, we were conscious of the dirt. And even more so of our grimy boots as we stepped onto the red Persian carpets lining the entry hall.

The flank of white tied butlers closed behind us. And as they moved, we reacted with instinct. Crystal hit the floor as we raised our guns with both hands, ready to fire. We did not like being surrounded, even by butlers holding silver trays of champagne. Tensions were high, mostly due to the confusion over the presence of the plantation and the unexpected army of butlers. It was clearly a different reality than what we had been living for several days as we crossed the jungle.

Then out of thin air, an elderly man appeared on the front porch. Despite his long grey hair, he did not look old or frail. In fact, he emanated power. He was muscular in build and massive in presence. The man had the air of nobility, not the dainty disposition of many European aristocrats.

He looked at us and smiled. The creases lifted the sides of his mouth, almost to his eyes, full of fire and authority.

With a commanding voice, not louder than a whisper, he said,

"Soyez bienvenue." (You are most welcome.)

With a small bow and a sweeping hand gesture, he invited us to go with him inside.

We lowered our guns but kept the safety catches off, still cautious, before we followed.

Why? He had just spoken our language, our dialect. In the middle of the jungle, in the middle of Africa. Now we were more curious than apprehensive.

Who was he?

————

The elderly gentleman was Monsieur Beaumont. He shared his story while showing us around his house. With champagne in one hand and gun in the other, my platoon and I listened.

Monsieur Beaumont was born and grew up in the Congo, on his parents' farm, not far from where we were. When he was a teenager, his parents sent him away to school in Belgium, believing their son needed to know his roots. He bitterly disagreed with them. He didn't come from Belgium. He came from Africa.

Heated arguments between his father and him resulted in a long self-imposed exile in Belgium, returning only to say goodbye to his father on his deathbed. After his father passed, there was no reason for him to live in Belgium. He was home again. He had forgotten how much he had missed his Africa. His home. His people.

As a lasting monument to his father, Monsieur Beaumont finished the construction of this mansion; it was a labor of love shared between them both. He told us of the very first time his father had spoke about building this house, when he was just a boy. And he recalled the years of architects, multiple plans, and then organizing all the materials needed to build. It took years but his father finally laid the foundation, right before he got sick.

While he continued to show us around, we could hear in his voice both the pride of the accomplishment and the love for his father, how much he missed him. We listened with rapt attention. I knew this name. But I could not place where I had heard it before.

The butlers continued to fill our glasses. Chilled sparkling champagne slid down my throat, a dreamlike sensation.

Monsieur Beaumont elaborated on the construction of the house. He spoke warmly of his estate back in Belgium, and how this house was fashioned as an exact replica. It was the dream of his father to bring the home of his birth to his adopted country, the Congo.

Every single piece of furniture, every glass, every plate came from Europe. Everything else was made from local materials. As we toured, he would pick up each piece, describing where it came from and how he got it here. Through the jungle. By foot and by air. Just like us.

We were struck by how bizarre it all was. But as he spoke, still commanding his butlers, the penny dropped and the puzzle pieces came together.

We all knew this house - it was a famous landmark back home. Because of the owners. And because of the story of the son.

If this was "that" house, if Beaumont was his last name, and if he was born here, and the fables were true...then we were in the presence of what many called:

The Belgian Tarzan.

Lagniappe

With this story, you must drink bubbles, of any kind: champagne, prosecco, cava, or apple juice with perrier. If you can
drink it in crystal flutes, all the better. (I still shake my head
thinking how surreal it all was: champagne in the Congo.)

As for a meal, I do not know if Tarzan would eat this; he probably would just have meat off the bone. Nor do I think that this
was served in the plantation home. However, it is a a simple
and wonderful Congolese recipe that you will use often: peanut
soup.

(For all you lovers of peanut butter, I love you too.)

Peanut Soup

20 minutes

2-3 cups of chicken stock
3 tablespoons olive oil
1 small onion, chopped
1 small green pepper/capsicum, chopped
2 cloves of garlic, crushed
Season with salt, black pepper, cayenne pepper
1 hot chilli, chopped
1 carrot, chopped
1-2 tomatoes, chopped or 1 can of tomatoes
¼ to ½ cup peanut butter (depends on you) (I say 'more is more').

1. Fry onion and garlic in oil on a medium heat for a few minutes until soft, add chilli cook for another few minutes.

2. Add capsicum and carrot, cook with lid on for 5 minutes until carrot is soft.

3. Add tomatoes, seasoning and stock. Stir and mix; cook with lid off for 15 minutes.

4. Stir in peanut butter. (If it becomes too thick, add more chicken stock.)

5. Place ¾ of soup in blender and blend until smooth, add to the rest of the soup. This way it keeps a bit of the 'chunkiness' of the soup and less veloute.

Try beer or a chilled red wine with this dish. Yum.

"Anything that gets your blood racing is probably worth doing."

Hunter Thompson

PLAYING CHICKEN IN TURKEY

Turkey

"This is the life!" I was just loving it. I was in Bodrum with my partner, sitting at a cafe, drinking coffee while basking in the sun.

"Isn't this wonderful?" Fredrik agreed as he sipped and smiled. He was still laughing over our hilarious attempts to buy bus tickets. It had been a comedy show. Nobody understood anyone but it all worked out in the end. International charades is always handy.

After enjoying weeks in Bodrum, we were ready for our next stop: Istanbul. I could hardly wait. I had fallen in love with Turkey and was eager to visit her capital.

After purchasing the tickets, we decided to store our bags on the bus so that we could freely walk around, savoring the last few hours here. Everything was organized. Just the way I like it.

I looked down at my watch to check. Four hours left; we had plenty of time.

I leaned back in my chair, stretched my hands over my head and looked out over the water. Glorious.

"This is the good life."

We had our tickets.
Our bags were on the bus.
We were enjoying the sun.
Bodrum had been good to us.

We were relaxed.
Everything was set.

What could possibly go wrong?

———————

With plenty of time to spare, we got to the bus depot. And started to look for our bus.

"Uhm, Fredrik?" I turned to my friend, who was busy taking the last pictures of Bodrum.

"Yeah, Ian?" He looked at me quizzically. "What's wrong?"

I had this creeping sensation go up my back. It is a chill starting at the base of your spine and instantly curdling your nerve endings, a kind of reverse nausea. Where you swallow involuntarily. Gulping air, before the the panic kicks in.

Fredrik was calm. He had not understood what I was beginning to.

We had walked to the middle of the depot where several buses were waiting to depart to different parts of Turkey. Including the one that was supposed to take us to Istanbul. Except it was not there. Our bus was not there. Fredrik grabbed my arm.

Panic had set in.

Under different circumstances, missing a bus would not mean anything. However, today there was a small hitch. A kicker.

Our bags were on that bus.
With everything.
Money.
Passports.
Clothes.
Camera.
And our tickets home.

Looking back at that moment, I think I swore. In fact, I know I swore.
So much for my tan.

Because I went white.

—————

"What are we going to do?" Fredrik asked.

I saw the group of men that had helped us to buy the ticket earlier. They were still there laughing and smoking amongst themselves. Rushing over to them, I thought to myself: thank god that there's someone that I recognize. I hoped they recognized us, because otherwise this would be difficult. What we thought was funny several hours before was no longer. We needed to be understood in order to find out where our bus had gone.

From looking at our faces, they saw the panic and easily understood what we needed. Information that our bus had left an hour before.

Holy baklava.
I swore again.
This is not optimal.

I don't know why but they wanted to help. We might have been paralyzed with panic but they definitely were not. They suddenly sprang into action. Like a bunch of mustached fairy godmothers.

Zip.
Zip.
Done.

Before you knew it, they found a 'pumpkin': a taxi came racing around the corner, screeching to a stop right in front of us. Our savior. It was amazing how quickly they had arranged it. Without knowing us, they helped to find a taxi and a driver to help catch up to the bus and get our stuff back.

All we needed was speed and that is what they had arranged. The taxi was a tin can which thought it was a Ferrari, and the driver was an elderly toothless man who thought he was Schumacher. I didn't care. Grateful, we were amazed with their graciousness. Off we went.

We zoomed towards the next bus stop, an hour away. At the speed that he was going, we would be there in 30 minutes. We were going fast.
White knuckle fast.
Drag racing through the first few curves, we thought that maybe the stress of the bags could be overshadowed by our death defying driving.

"You ok?" Schumacher asked us while smiling over his shoulder in order to check and reassure us.

We both nodded.
I urged him on.
Fredrik made the sign of the cross.

———

The first stop came quickly. It was guarded by a man sitting on a chair outside. There was no sign.
No table.
No toilets.
And most importantly, no bus.

No matter.

We did not expect to catch the bus so early on our journey, but we asked if he could radio ahead and tell the bus driver to wait for us. Our fingers were crossed that the guard would do this for us. He did, and we raced onwards. Faster. If that was possible. It was if this was Le Mans, throughout the countryside of Turkey. Up and down hills, around mountains. Schumacher was insistent we were going to catch the bus. I was positive he was telling the truth because, by now, we were going faster than the speed of light.

The second stop felt like it was almost around the bend.
Still no bus.
But there were chickens.
This bus guard did have teeth.
And he had a table and a bus sign to sit under.
It was progress.
I felt that we were getting places. We were closer at least.

Again, we raced to our third stop.
This place had a toilet.
And more chickens.
And more people.

Which was lovely. In fact, they were all lovely. Every one of them had been made aware of our race to catch this bus. We drove faster than I had ever seen on a Formula I track. The guards of each stop were phoning ahead in hopes to stall the bus.

Our fingers were crossed.

But our good fortune would only take us so far. Suddenly, I heard a giant sounding "pop". Our drag racing through the countryside of Turkey came to a temporary stop when the taxi's worn out tires met a deep ditch.

Now, normally anywhere else in the world, this would be of concern. Changing tires or finding another taxi takes precious time. But with the help of the bus depot guards and the villagers who were aware of our situation, within moments - I kid you not - another pumpkin arrived on the scene to help us.

Zip.
Zap.
Done.

We bid farewell to 'Toothless Schumacher' and his Turkish Ferrari, and said hello to the Turkish version of 'Chitty Chitty Bang Bang'.

Somehow, the 2 of us squeezed into the taxi with 6 other people. Somehow, we also managed to find space for several chickens. Getting into the taxi took acrobatic flexibility. I didn't know whose hands were whose or how to breathe with all the feathers in the air. It was crazy.

"Go forth!" Fredrik battle cried while laughing. I must say that one had to be careful laughing. A feather might go down the wrong throat.

You could inhale dust, gas, or chicken feathers. Your pick.

I didn't mind.
I was having the time of my life.
It was hilarious.

We did not go as fast as Toothless Schumacher, probably because of the weight. But when we got to the next stop, we were greeted by the entire town. We were famous; the grapevine must have been working. Albeit it had not yet successfully stopped the bus, but every little village along the way knew of us. The townspeople were waiting on the side of the road to cheer us on.

I always wanted to be famous.
I definitely looked famous as I got out of the taxi with chicken feathers in my hair.

However, despite the celebrity status, there was no time to waste. No time for autographs or making new friends and a fan base.

Off we went.
We were so close.
The bus had been there only ten minutes before.

However, this was the final stop for Chitty Chitty Bang Bang. We needed another taxi and before we knew it, the Turkish people provided another pumpkin. This one had a working radio with the volume on high. It definitely felt loud, probably because the boombox took up the entire back seat.

The best news was that this taxi was slightly faster.
Maybe because the taxi was lighter.
It had fewer people and fewer chickens.
There were only the three of us and a boom box.

We drove across the country at breakneck speed. Which was great because we could finally see the bus ahead.

Success was near.
Our bags were almost in our possession.
Now, if we could only get the bus to stop.
We would have to pass the bus in order to hail it down.

Small problem though: we were on the side of a cliff.
And there were cars coming in the opposite direction.
On a one lane highway.

"Stopppp!" We were going to have to scream it down. And scream we did.

Fredrik was leaning over the taxi driver to honk the horn, yelling to the bus. The passengers saw us and started screaming "Stop" to their bus driver.
Our taxi driver was screaming.
Even the chickens were screaming.

What was I doing, you ask? I was literally hanging out of the window of the taxi, banging on the side of the bus, whispering. (No, just joking. I was screaming too.) Fredrik was not only leaning on the car horn, he was holding onto my legs so I would not fall.

Bang!
Bang!
Stop!
Bang!

Cars were coming in the opposite direction.
Where were they going to go?
I did not think about death or the imminent collision.
I did not think about falling in between the cars.
All I wanted was the bus to stop.

Finally, it did.
The bus stopped.
My heart started again.

Whew.

———

Immediately, the screaming and the yelling from moments before turned into cheers and jubilation. Everyone was clapping. Everyone was happy that we had made it. Everyone was patting us on the back. They were kissing us. Congratulating us. It was a party. On the side of the road.

On the side of a cliff. Traffic stopped to join in on the celebration.

Everyone was hugging: the bus driver, the taxi driver, the passengers. I even patted the chickens on the head, I was that happy. It was a success story, a happy ending for everyone.

Our journey had become their journey.
Our trial was their trial.
Our success was their success.

The Turkish people were there to help us every step of the way. They were singing in happiness and yelling for the bus to stop, joining in the struggle, helping people they had never met. They might not have tables, but if you needed help, they had 'pumpkins' and 'tin can' taxis which flew across the country. You might be strangers to them but you were invited in as family.

Those who had nothing helped those they did not know. They did everything they could to help. They are amazing people, the Turks. So much heart.

Our chase was probably not for the faint of heart, however that being said, we only met people with lots of it.

———————

Lagniappe

Turkish coffee is a must. Every country in the Middle East will say it is *their* coffee: the Greeks call it Greek coffee; the Turks call it Turkish coffee, the Arabs call it Arabic coffee. A loved child has many names...

Turkish Coffee
10 minutes

1 cup water (Use cold water only.)
1 tablespoon extra fine ground coffee
⅛ ground cardamom
As much sugar as you like

1. Bring water and sugar to boil in a small saucepan or saucier.
2. Remove from heat and stir in coffee and cardamom.
3. Bring mixture to boil again, constantly stirring.
4. Remove from heat when it foams.
5. Return to heat after it simmers down in order to foam again.
6. Pour into cup; do not stir again.

Some cultures will serve this with dates on the side for the extra bite of sugar or a cinnamon stick for extra flavor.

I chose a recipe that is super easy to do. It is a great salad for the summer nights and takes no time at all to prepare. You have probably had it before but little did you know that you have been enjoying a little bit of Turkish culture all this time.

Turkish Salad

15 minutes

1½ cup diced tomatoes
1 cup diced green bell pepper
1 cup diced peeled cucumber
½ cup minced fresh parsley
⅓ cup green onion
¼ cup fresh lemon juice
2 tablespoons water
1 tablespoon olive oil
¼ teaspoon salt
⅛ teaspoon fresh ground pepper

1. This dish is ridiculously simple. Combine all the ingredients and chill for an hour before serving.

Note: Color me crazy but sometimes I exchange the tomatoes for watermelon. It is not Turkish, I know, I know. But still good and equally refreshing. And skip the coffee for this salad. Have chilled prosecco instead.

Steel Magnolia:

noun / stel - mag-ˈnōl-yə
(chiefly southern U.S.)

- A woman who possesses
  the strength of steel yet the
  gentleness of a magnolia.

- A woman who exemplifies both
  traditional femininity as well
  as an uncommon fortitude.

CONFESSIONS OF A HAIRDRESSER

Algeria

There was a time when I did not wash my own hair. I don't think I bought shampoo for almost a year.

Shocked? You must think that I was absolutely filthy. Which could not be further from the truth.

For many years, I lived in countries where I could get a wash and blow dry for $2.

I saw it as a double bingo with a bonus. For one, there was the glamor. I felt glamorous. (Who doesn't after having spent time at the hairdressers?) This was also my armor. While reporting on degeneracy, chaos and humanitarian tragedy, feeling glamorous was my armor. My insides might be torn apart, my soul might be crying, but I needed some semblance of control, if only for show. If only by a thread. Or in my case, a hair strand. And finally, at the hairdressers, I found a sisterhood, a battalion of heart warriors and soothsayers, cheerleaders, and comedians.

You see, it was never about the hair. And it was never about the 2 dollars. It was about the sisterhood. No matter where I come from or what I believe in, I belong to a sisterhood. A global one.

———

For a few years, I had been working as a journalist while living in a war zone of land mines of truth, destroying the ideological landscape of my youth. The life I led, the questions I asked were not always compatible with what I thought was right or good. There is no black. There is no white. Grey is an illusion.

Existing like this for an extended period of time wears and tears threads of sanity. In shifting sands of reality, preconceived ideas were constantly challenged with the faces that dropped atomic bombs of truth, contrary to those told me as I grew up.

I needed an anchor. I needed armor. I needed something to keep me together while my world was falling apart. I knew that reconstruction would be lengthy and the journey would be long. The threads keeping me together were worn and I needed something to hold me together. Time was something I did not have.

So, I chose a different solution. If I looked like I had it together, then the world of prying eyes and false sympathy would leave my healing to do its job in silence. I was going to focus on the 'wrapping paper' not the 'content' inside, postponing that surgery for another time. Wrapping paper for women is very simple: hair, nails, and clothes.

(I am not the only one that employs this feeble trick, procrastinating the healing the soul. Ask any woman how she is. And if she answers, "I'm fine," and looks it, you can be 100% sure she is the exact opposite. This might seem confusing to many men, but to many women, it makes perfect sense. We do not have time to fall apart.)

———

Back to the story.

Algiers was in the middle of a revolution, one of power and of culture. Consequences of the clash are never contained. The effects were visible everywhere, how the clash raged on in silence, in degradation, on faces of people and buildings.

Every other day while I was there, I would go to the local hairdressers: Yasmine's. She had a small room on the fourth floor in a worn down building in the center of downtown Algiers, built during the many years of French colonisation. But since the days of the Algerian Revolution, the building had never been renovated, like many others in the capital. The white paint was now yellow, the shutters were broken, and the wear and tear of life were visible.

If the outside was run down, the inside was pristine clean. These women might not have money or control over the upkeep of the building, but they did have soap and water. It was such a testament to pride and hard work, the resilience in the worst of times, to make sure their place of commerce was welcoming and clean. I was inspired every time I walked in the building. And was in awe. Dignity and pride have a special kind of shine. The kind that brightens up everyone's day.

The little room was constantly flooded with the sandy gold light, native to countries that border the Mediterranean. Naturally, there were mirrors everywhere, which only accentuated the lightness in the room. Old black and white pictures of Hollywood actresses, tinged yellow with age, donned the aquamarine walls. Rai music was continuously playing in the background, hair dryers always blasting, and the symphony of soprano voices would rise and fall in Arabic and in French. The floor was cement. (This made it easier to clean, first with a broom and then to hose down with water. I loved the practicality of it all.) Plastic red buckets full of water were standing ready for the wash. In the corner, there was a tea station. An electric water boiler. A sack of sugar and a bundle of mint bought every day at the market. There were tea cups everywhere. Mint tea was prolific. The balm of the mint, sugar and tea leaves refreshed the body of every tired soul that slumped into Yasmine's chair.

Her place was an oasis. In the truest sense, it was a place to replenish, far from the maddening crowd. In French, there is a verb which when interpreted means: to be gain strength from the source. That is how I like to describe Yasmine's establishment. You came weak, you left strong.

How was this possible? What made hers different from any

other place? I am sure that there are many, if not a million, other hairdresser shops, giving the same gift, transforming the weary into a being of beauty. The soul feels the comfort and support that comes from being surrounded by women who acknowledge the pain, the struggle of life, and despite it all, celebrate it with laughter shining through tears. The heart beats lighter, the burden is carried by many and not by one alone.

———

My first time at Yasmine's, I was immediately greeted as a long lost sister. A cup of mint tea was soon put in my hands, along with smiles that reached the eyes and warmed the heart.

Who could refuse such a welcome? These beautiful women were laughing and dancing. Their long dresses followed their every movement, a rainbow of cloth. Some working behind the chairs, some sitting playing cards, some waiting for their turn. Each woman possessed a rich sensuality, balancing their character of warriors and tender healing hearts. You could see all this from one look. The women of the Maghreb are phenomenal.

Here at Yasmine's, I joined a citizenship of sisterhood I had never known. And before long, I was welcomed into their land of confidences.

As I sat, I was invited to listen to their stories and share my own. Each woman contributed her own tale. These were more than stories. These were confessions of the heart. The bleeding heart. The stomped heart. The broken heart. The mended heart. The healing one and the one in the ICU. Each story would break my heart. And ironically, put it back together. Tragic yet healing.

To this day, those stories affect me. These women experienced the arc of tragedy and tribulation: buried children, surrounded by death, health limitations, physical pain, and sometimes raped, abused, beaten by their husbands, by their family members, by their neighbors, by the soldiers. But at the end of every story: these women would rise. Even with their money stolen, their identities forsaken, opportunities left behind - they would get up, pick up the pieces of their heart and move forward, believing in a better life. They would get up every day, again and again. To take care of their children. To answer the promise they made to their God, to their families, and finally to themselves. These women would stand up to the bullying, aggression and violence. They would push themselves off the floor, spitting blood, and continue on. They would rise. Again. And again.

Some of them came to Yasmine's to get help and it was given. They fled and moved to another country. Some others stayed behind to take care of their children. The choice was never easy. The sacrifice was always made by the victim.

There were stories told which were decades old, and others that happened a few days before. For me, hearing their confessions obliterated what I thought strength looked like. Literally, they would tell their tale, discuss it, cry, and then laugh. And finally, they would dance. It was the arc of humanity. In its purest form of perseverance. "I will not only survive. I will also dance."

I know that there are hairdressers like this everywhere in the world. Yasmine's was not the only one I visited. Of course, similar experiences are not limited to the walls of beauty salons. I know that this kind of sisterhood is not rare. In every country, in every town, on every street, there are kitchens full. It is where beauty is more than skin deep, where awesome strength is not physical, where the disappointments and tragedies are shared, and burdens are lightened.

Where laughter replaces the tears and you dance to the tune of a broken heart.

Yet still. And always.

And again.

You rise to dance.

Knowing you are not alone.

Lagniappe

Mint Tea

This story calls for mint tea, which is Liptons tea served with 1 or 2 or 3 spoons of sugar and fresh mint. Literally, you put fresh mint into black sugar tea. No milk. No lemon. And none of this prefab stuff. Old school is the right school as far as drinking traditional mint tea goes.

An extra bonus: should you like it chilled, do as they do in Saudi Arabia: increase the concentrate by leaving the tea to steep for 10 - 15 minutes. Allow enough time for it to chill. Serve with apple juice and sparking water. If you want a little more kick, then use cider. It is what many Saudis serve as non-alcoholic champagne.

Algerian Garlic Shrimp

Time: 10 minutes

I chose this dish because if I could get it every day, I would have it every day. Nothing is better than fresh shrimp with garlic and chili. Unbelievably good. Simple. Easy. Great for summer. Or whenever you can get fresh shrimp. Which is a daily basis should you live in any of the coastal towns of Algeria.

You serve it with a cold beer or chilled white wine. Do not forget to serve with slices of french baguette. Believe me, you will want to dip the bread into the sauce after you have eaten all the shrimp.

2.5 pounds of shrimp, cleaned, deveined, heads intact
1 bulb of garlic, diced
¼ cup extra virgin olive oil
1 tomato, diced
1 teaspoon cumin
½ teaspoon coriander
½ teaspoon sweet paprika
1 teaspoon harissa or chili paste
½ lemon, juice

1. Mash everything in a mortar bowl. Add more olive oil if it seems to be more paste than sauce.

2. Add the shrimp and mix the shrimp into the sauce, using your clean hands or a spoon. This way, you make sure that the sauce in every shrimp.

3. Empty the entire mixture on the olive oil coated iron skillet, on medium high heat. When the shrimp turn pink, they are ready.

Enjoy. I know you will.

"Footloose, Footloose, kick off your Sunday shoes…"

Kenny Loggins

BARNYARD IN BEIJING

China

The room swayed. Literally, it swayed with humanity. At least, it looked like the entire room was moving, from the floor to the rafters. Probably because there were 150 couples on the dance floor, do-si-do-ing, stomping their feet as they turned in a large circle.

There was a 10 piece band playing on the stage, belting out one country classic after another. Everyone was dressed in matching traditional Western apparel, complete with cowboy boots, large metal belt buckles, and fringed calico shirts. Their cowboy hats moved together, in sync with the beat.

The dance hall was a renovated opera house theater with the extra high ceilings, box seats for small groups, and a balcony on the first floor encircling the dance pit.

You could not help but be moved by the music and the electricity in the air. Besides, I loved the smell of wood and sawdust. This was country dancing at its best. Barnyard, booze, and boots. My kind of night. I was itching to dance, my feet tapping to the music and my hips swinging to the beat. All I needed was a partner. You know what they say: "save the horse"...So, I made a move to the floor to find me a cowboy.

It was a great Friday night. One that you would expect in any small town across America, especially Texas.

However, I was not in the Lone Star State. Or any other state in the United States.

I was in Beijing.

And I was the only Westerner there.

———————

Earlier that night, my friends and I went to a posh restaurant, blinged to the max and dressed to the nines in high heels and short skirts. We started at the bar and ordered a few cosmopolitans to wash back the Beijing smog. Don't get me wrong. We loved Beijing and moreover didn't mind the smog. (Raise your hand if you smoke.)

We were looking for a well deserved time-out from the hustle and bustle of the week. Isn't that what Friday nights are for? All over the world?

Before long, tired eyes became eyes full of mischief. We laughed at the jokes we told each other: bad, cheeky, and more bad ones. (I always laugh before I get to the punch line.) Leaving the bar, we went to sit down for dinner. Nothing like breakfast at night when you can have dim sum. (Dim Sum is Chinese breakfast, just in case you were wondering. I never knew that before I came to China.) It goes without saying, I skipped the shark fin soup and went straight for the dumplings.

After licking our fingers and emptying the bottle, we left the restaurant and crammed into a taxi, now in the mood for some glitter action and disco dancing. Knocking on the bulletproof glass that separated us in the car, I introduced myself to our cab driver, Mr. Li. I was new to Beijing and did not know where to go and needed his help. I am a great believer that all taxi drivers are better than priests: they keep the best secrets of the city. They know everything. The confessions they could tell.

And in this instance, the secret I wanted was the best place to go dancing in Beijing.

Now, my Mandarin is pretty rusty. I struggle with the 9 consonants necessary to master Mandarin, at least in order to be understood. I have never been able to differentiate between the multiple syllables. It all sounds the same to me: ts, tz, sz...

But like every American college boy in Tijuana after two cervezas, I can tell you after several cosmopolitans, I was fluent in Chinese. I was queen of the consonants.

Yup. That would probably explain a lot of what happened later. I could have been ignorantly blissful, but I thought Mr. Li and I understood each other. Or at least connected, since he nodded in agreement after multiple minutes of my rambling and sign language. Looking back, I think I looked like a chicken squawking when I tried to sign language "dancing". He closed his bullet proof partition before turning around to start his car. And off we were.

Hopefully, to Studio 54.

Now, if you have ever been in the backseat of a taxi with girls between dinner and dancing, you know there will be a few moments of lip gloss application, skirt adjusting, dirty jokes, and the occasional spontaneous karaoke. Pitch perfect we were not, but ABBA had never sounded so good. I think we sang better than Agnetha and Bjorn. The acoustics in a old Chinese taxi, rambling down the main streets of Beijing in the middle of the night, are beyond the pale. Equal to any recording studio.

Or at least our Chinese cabbie thought so. He didn't mind chirping in. It was truly a bonding moment, singing "Dancing Queen" with Mr. Li.

Before long, it seemed that we had arrived at our surprise destination. Mr. Li turned to drop us off in front of a big building which looked like an old opera house. There was a line of people outside, waiting to get in. And the accompanying mini traffic jam due to all the cars randomly parked around the building. These are good signs for a great place. At least in my experience. This place looked like it must be the place in Beijing.

Maybe my Mandarin was not so shabby after all. One thing I was sure of: cabbies know it all. My belief was reinforced that cabbies know the best that every city has to offer.

Trusty Chinese cabbie: Mr. Li.

After paying him, we blew kisses goodbye to Mr. Li before taking our places in line, right next to the bouncer. After a few minutes standing in the cold, we finally got in. We were ready to get down and boogie.

Operative word: boogie.

However, this was no Studio 54. This was no hip hop nation. Nope. Not even Chinese opera. No sugar pop Filipino band. No backstreet bush bar neither. Nada. Nope. There was no boogie happening here.

What we saw made our jaws drop. It was an huge theater full of hundreds of Chinese couples, all of them line-dancing to Dolly Parton.

They were not only line-dancing; they were stomping the ground, and slapping hands. Every single dancer was dressed up in Country-Western-Friday- Night-Light clothes. Calico in every color. Boots in alligator. Buckles the size of fists. Imagine a room of hundreds of Chinese, every single one wearing cowboy hats. There was even hay on the floor.

Hay. On. The. Floor.

We looked at each other in shock. Shrugging our shoulders, flipping our hair, we walked laughing to the dance floor, giving it our best Solid Gold entrance in our mini skirts and heels.

Because when in Rome...

Or when in Beijing...

Act like you're back home...

Hee-haw!

———————

Lagniappe

Have your favorite Friday night cocktail, of course.

As for a recipe, um, silly if you thought I was going to give you the recipe to anything other than Peking Duck. I mean, seriously, it is duck made in Beijing. It is so good. And although you might think it is difficult to make, it really is not.

Peking Duck

10 hours. But wait! Don't freak out. 9 hours and 50 minutes of these you are sleeping…

1 whole duck, 6 pounds
sea salt & freshly ground white pepper
6 tablespoons honey
4 tablespoons Chinese five-spice powder
3 tablespoons dark soy sauce, divided
2 tablespoons brown sugar
1 tablespoon cornstarch
6 tablespoons hoisin sauce
6 tablespoons sugar
2 tablespoons sesame oil
scallions and cucumber, chopped to garnish.

1. Clean the duck. (I hope you are doing that with all the recipes.) Sprinkle the duck with salt and pepper, pat in, and leave it in the roasting pan until ready to cook.

2. Mix in a bowl: honey, water, Chinese five-spice, 2 tablespoons of the soy sauce, and the brown sugar.

3. Brush the duck all over, inside and out. Leave to dry and then repeat until you have used almost of all the mixtures. Leave it to marinate over night, uncovered in the fridge.

4. Next day, in preheated 350°F oven, cook for 45 minutes while basting with the leftover glaze/mixture. You will

see that the skin will start to become crispy and brown. Just make sure that it does not start to burn or get too dark.

5. Meanwhile, mix cornstarch with 1 tablespoon of water. This is the base for the sauce.

6. In a pan, heat the hoisin, sugar, sesame oil, and remaining soy sauce. When it is mixed, fold in the cornstarch mixture. Stir so it thickens. Yum. When you see it thicken and you can hear the duck crisping in the oven, you know you are in for a good time.

Serve the duck and the sauce while topping with chopped scallions or cucumbers. I like it plain and simple. So good.

"It was the best of times, it was the worst of times, it was the age of wisdom, it was the age of foolishness, ...we were all going direct to Heaven, we were all going direct the other way..."

Charles Dickens
A Tale of Two Cities

Keep the Caviar

Iran

With the butt of one AK-47 in the stomach and feeling the butt of another in my back, my hands slowly went up.

Sighing, I turned. I was getting way too used to this. In fact, I was bored with it all now. Guns everywhere. Some being pointed at you and some being fired.

Thankfully, they had not been fired at me, yet.

"What do you want?" I asked. Whatever would make the men happy, I would get. All I wanted was to get home. And I was almost there, at the airport, I had never been so close.

Overstaying my welcome might be considered an understatement. I had come for one week of business. It was supposed to be easy. Meet, greet and then go home. No problems. No surprises.

What I did not expect was a revolution.

The Iranian Revolution.

———

When the first shots were fired, I was staying at the finest hotel in Tehran. Insurgents quickly occupied it, keeping us hostage. One by one, we were brought into the main lobby so that they could keep track of us.

As fantastic as I am, all ego aside, I knew that they were not looking for me. I knew that my dealings in Tehran were all above board and legal. However, there was an uneasy feeling that perhaps I had unintentionally upset someone. I doubted that had happened but you could never be too sure. Especially in this place. And during this time.

Revolutions are never clean.

The uneasy feeling could also be because the hotel lobby was full of machine guns held by trigger happy Iranians. No one knew what to think. I sure didn't. I had never been political and was not going to start now.

Let me put it this way. I do not speak Farsi. I speak Survival.

And in a series of staggered English, German, and sign language, I learned that there was a guest in the hotel who was close to the Shah. How close? Like family.

When I heard his name, I laughed. And then wiped my brow as I exhaled. This was good because I knew him. We had met at the hotel bar on my first night in Tehran and both of us had a fondness for, let's say, the finer things in life. I had introduced him to my favorite cocktail, a home run with the ladies: half champagne and half cognac. It was called "Caesar's Drink", an ambrosia for the gods and Emperors of Rome.

At least, I felt like one every time I drank it. And so did the ladies. My newfound friend did not need it so much. Let me rephrase that. He did not need a drink to make him feel like a Caesar. As a Pahlavi, he was one already.

Needless to say, we bonded.

Being in the presence of a Pahlavi changed my circumstances. I was now under imperial protection, along with the rest of his entourage. The Iranians that surrounded us were not there to overthrow but to guard. And by protecting him in this hotel, we were all protected from the chaos that took place downstairs and outside.

They called it protection. Actually, it was a nice word for house arrest on the penthouse floor. I was going to be the last person to argue, happy to stay put until it was safe to leave the hotel and to take my plane home. Or any plane home. Especially the last plane home.

There were benefits to house arrest with a member of the ruling class. Apart from the ever present machine guns, who was I to argue with a 5 star hotel stocked with champagne, cognac, and caviar?

Certainly not me.

If you were going to be in a revolution, champagne and caviar is the diet of choice. You could say, it takes the edge off.

And "room service revolution" definitely has a ring to it, don't you think? No better words could describe the five days we spent together. I will not go into details. However, I will say when I got bored, I spoon fed caviar to the women.

What can I say? I wanted to keep the forks clean. It was a revolution, after all.

————

Sadly, all good things must come to an end, even being held hostage during a revolution. We were escorted to the airport. Every one of us keen to get home.

After checking in, I took my hand luggage and went through security. Nothing like being escorted through security that had security. I had gotten a seat on the last flight out of Tehran, and to get on this flight, each of us had to pass through 14 rounds of security checks. Just to be sure. They all had their machine guns ready, their nuzzles guiding me through checkpoint. Some soldiers patted me down and others checked my hand luggage.

Again and again. 13 times.

There was not much in my briefcase: papers, passport, book, pens. You know, the usual. And caviar, of course. Mementos were necessary. I was bringing champagne and caviar home with me. (What else? Please don't say t-shirt.)

Caviar, however, was against the sensibilities of the new Iranian regime. Shouting in Farsi, the soldier took the caviar out of my briefcase, telling me that it was outlawed.

Instinctively, I reached for it, a big no-no when surrounded by armed revolutionaries.

"What do you want?" I asked. Looking at angry faces jabbing their guns in my stomach and back.

"Keep the champagne," I offered to the Shia revolutionary. "Just don't take the caviar."

"Please, let me keep the caviar."

———————

There are times when you make a point, there are times when you defend the principle, and then there are times when it is really not worth your life. The plane I was about to board was the last one out of Tehran. And getting into an argument over caviar would probably keep me from getting on that plane and most definitely: living.

Bowing my head to the armed revolutionaries, I picked up the can of caviar, dropped it in the garbage and continued on to the next check. And then the next one after that. And the next one after that.

13 more times.

Each of us had to go through 14 checks before getting to the airport lounge, where I sat down and waited to board. The first thing I noticed was total silence. You could hear a pin drop. Everyone was quiet. Apprehension and fear were transparent. We had all received strict orders to be on our best behavior, especially until we were out of Iranian airspace. No one was going to make trouble. It was literally "on pain of death" or else. No more planes were ever leaving Tehran when it was still the capital city of the Kingdom of Iran. This was our last chance.

This was the last plane.

We boarded in silence. We looked at each other in silence. We strapped in silence. Once again, armed guards came on board to check us. Body pat down, bag search, and passport check. Everyone complied. And no one said a word.

Not even as they disembarked the plane and shut the doors. Nor when we began to taxi off. There was total silence in the plane.

And not a word was spoken when we began to lift off. Not much breathing was done either.

After flying for a while, the overhead speaker crackled. Interrupting the complete silence we had been in. Were we going to turn around? Would we be shot out of the air? Anything could happen. And no one knew. We had never felt so vulnerable.

Finally, we heard the voice of the pilot. We held our breath.

And then exhaled as he announced, "Ladies and Gentlemen, we have now left Iranian airspace."

I do not remember what he said next. Why? Because I could not hear it. The plane had gone from tomb silence to the loudest of festivals. The jubilation was enormous. The anxiety was gone.

Exhaling and exhilarated, I was shaking hands and hugging my fellow passengers. It was a party and I had something to contribute.

I reached into my bag and got out the second can. Opening it up, I turned to the man seated to my right and extended it to him,

"Caviar?"

===========

Lagniappe

Nice work if you can get it, but most of us humans cannot afford caviar however I would suggest that you try toasted pita bread with taramasalata with champagne or prosecco. It is a poor man's version of caviar but equally as tasty. Most supermarkets will hold all of these ingredients and it literally takes no time at all, only the time to toast.

If you do feel like cooking, I have added a recipe for a refreshing ginger drink along with the recipe for a glorious Persian kabob. Ah, delicious.

Enjoy.

Ginger Sekanjabin
15 minutes

This drink is hugely refreshing. And so good. An Iranian favorite of all time.

4 cups white sugar
2½ cups water
1 cup white wine vinegar
½ cup minced fresh ginger

1. Boil sugar and water together over high heat for 2 to 3 minutes.
2. Remove the pan from the heat and stir in vinegar and ginger.
3. Allow mixture to cool and then strain and store. Done!

To use: stir ratio of 1 part syrup to 4 part water, flat or carbonated; serve cold with ice.

Persian Kabob

30 minutes

Grill: high heat

8 ounce (1 container) plain low-fat yoghurt
1 onion chopped
½ teaspoon dried mint
Season with: salt, pepper, juice of ½ lemon, juice of two cloves of garlic
2 pounds beef top sirloin, cut into large cubes

1. Mix yoghurt, onion, and mint together. Season with salt, pepper, and lemon. Add garlic if you desire extra flavor.

2. Place meat into mixture. Cover for 6 hours to marinate.

3. Place meat on skewers and grill, turning every 10 minutes.

Serve with cucumber salad. (You can also keep the marinade and blend it for a side dip. No need to waste the good stuff.)

"Wild thing,
I think I love you."

Chip Taylor

THREE DAYS IN THE AMAZON

Brazil

Well, that was nuclear surprise. My fiancée turned to me at the lawyer's office and said, "I didn't know you were married before."

"Uhm. I am not. I have not." Stuttering, my brain was going into overdrive. I was married? No, this is a joke. Seriously, this is something that I would remember. Right? Dress, confetti... man? These are things that no woman forgets since the beginning of Cinderella. It is not like misplacing my keys or my phone. This was a person. A live real person that I happened to forget.

Turning to the lawyer, "Could you give me more details. Like who?" Good grief. I understand doing a thorough background check before marriage but this was over and above the call of duty - for any lawyer. The zealousness of whom was probably in line with his benefactor: my fiancé's mother.

God bless her.

Not.

Grabbing Michael's hand, I looked at him and said "You know me, I have never ever ever been married before. I swear it. On my mother's grave, on my grandparents' grave, on our future children's birth."

"I. Have. Never. Been. Married. Before."

"Yes, you have," the lawyer looked at me. "In Brazil."

Head rolled back. Eyes followed. I remembered. The hut. The tea. The pipe. The smell. The heat. The monkeys. The shaman. The Indians. The butterflies. The Amazon.

And the man.

"I was only there for three days!"

That did not sound like "no".

———————

Personally, I blame the monkeys. I could also blame the tea. But that comes later. But really, honestly, I blame the monkeys for this mess. You know, those furry, limber, little humans that walk on all fours and jump and swing in trees like the Jungle Book? Yes, those monkeys. I just so happen to think that they are the cutest things ever. I went to the Amazon because of them.

Flashback to my college days, when my boyfriend of two years started talking about taking a trip up the Amazon river. My first response was no. A firm "no".

Why? Because I had just watched a show about piranhas. And I saw how they gobbled up a piece of meat in milliseconds. And that was not happening to me. Because with Murphy's law, I would be the one to fall out of the boat while happily rowing up the Amazon River. And within seconds, I would be gobbled up by these tiger-fanged fish. Nope. My answer was "no".

Do not get me wrong. I love to travel. But look at it this way, some people prefer not to be in the same room as spiders. Or snakes. Or swim with sharks. This can determine what choice you make. And in my case, travel is not the question, survival is. As a warm blooded mammal, I prefer not to swim in the same body of water as piranhas. Call me freaky. But no.

Christian knew of my love of monkeys so he changed tactics. He started to talk about rowing up the Amazon river with monkeys swinging over our heads. Before long, I changed my mind. Who could resist going into the jungle of the Amazon with the king character of the Jungle Book?

Excitement took over and I went to pack my bags. What can I say? Christian was persuasive. And I was about to find out persuasive he could be.

After a long plane ride, we landed in Sao Paulo. Upon collecting our luggage, we immediately started to make arrangements to fly into the country where we would meet our guide. With our tickets booked for the following day, our next task was to find lodging for the night. (Yes, dear reader, we were not into planning in advance.)

By the time we found the hostel and left our bags, we were starving. Local food was definitely on the menu. And caipirinhas as the first course. 4 caipirinhas later, you could say we dived into living the great life that is Brazil.

Brazilians are amazing people. And even better dancers. In the beginning, I tried to learn by watching them. And then after a few drinks, I ventured out onto the dance floor. In comparison to the locals, my backbone is made of steel while theirs are made of rubber. The way they danced was hypnotizing. I had never seen people move their bodies like that.

I was going to have to take notes; if only to get better at sex. It was clear to me that dancing in Brazil looks a lot like foreplay. It was all an invitation. The heat. The sensuality. The dancing. The caipirinhas.

And I loved it. I was in love with Brazil.

The next morning we were both hungover and lethargic from the combination of flight and festivities. Trying to push us out of bed and out the door, Christian poured coffee down my throat while he guzzled water. To be fair, he did not really need to give me a lot of coffee. All he needed to do was say the magic word: Amazon. The lethargy vaporized and the hangover was gone by the time we got the airport and took off for the land of the monkeys.

And the land of another million animals. The Amazon rainforest holds 10% of all the species in the world. It is fascinating. I could not even begin to imagine what it would be like to live a few days surrounded all this nature, all these animals, and no people.

What was even more exciting was that we were about to enter the last realm of undisturbed humanity. The place where the planet had remained practically untouched since its birth, and where the people were untainted by forced evolution of modernity. I could not wait. It was as if we were offered the most sacred of opportunities to go back to where we were 'born'.

By the time we landed, drove to the port, and walked onto the docks, I was almost humming hymns, all in reverence to the great Mother, the great Amazon. I knew in my heart of hearts that I was starting a journey which would change my life.

I looked at Christian. Smiling, I took his hand. We both got in the boat.

And pushed off.

————

People, my people. I cannot tell you the wonder, the happiness, the ecstasy that comes from living your dream, when it just pounces on your back and literally takes the banana out of your hand before swinging back into the trees.

I screamed with delight. Or surprise. Or both. Or perhaps I squeaked loudly. But it was amazing. I had interacted with a monkey. And he with me. And I named him.

King Louie. Of course.

I told him that if he protected me from the piranhas, he could have more bananas. Louie is smart. He understands English. And I trust him. So, I gave him all the bananas I had. (I must admit that I bought them on purpose.)

Christian was laughing the entire time. Our guide, Tomo, was not pleased. He warned against our making friends with wild monkeys. He had a point, but I did not care.

We sailed on, further into the jungle. We sensed that the further into the Amazon we went, the more of ourselves we left behind. The lushness, the green, the water, the immersion of nature was welcomed. It literally surrounded us. I had never been accompanied by butterflies, but they followed me everywhere. It was if the Amazon knew I was coming and rolled out the red carpet to show off the wonders of Mother Nature.

It could be Mother Amazon knew I was coming, or that this is the way we were always supposed to live. One with our planet. With our surroundings. We breathe the same air. We inhabit the same ground and eat from the same soil. I entered into a new reverence for this earth that I 'visit'. That we all do.

As our boat took us further down the Amazon, as we immersed ourselves increasingly in nature, further and further away from "civilization", our conversations became increasingly philosophical. To break up the intensity, we would be silly, but most of the time, we were silent with wonder.

 Our days were full of discovery and our nights full of gratitude. Every day we would row deeper into the Amazon, knowing that we were still far from her very heart; the Amazon is huge and massive in its grandeur.

The sensations were overwhelming. The sights, the sounds, the smells. It was as if we had left a world of grey and entered into one of dazzling color. The lushness was palpable. We wanted to take it all in. Like a religious convert. To life and nature itself.

Frequently, after setting up camp at night, the only way to absorb the beautiful unfamiliarity surrounding us was to join in the silence of nature and drink in the stars. We were unable to speak. We could only feel.

Tomo was the supreme guide: patient with our questions, proud of his home, and probably more knowledgeable than most National Geographic editors. We deemed ourselves extremely fortunate to have him.

As an unexpected treat, we were going to stop at Tomo's village. After five days, Christian and I could not wait to meet his family and see his home. We had heard his stories and knew that this was a once-in-a-lifetime opportunity. On top of that, we were going to meet his shaman.

I had never met a shaman. I had met a priest. Once. A long time ago. But that was it. A shaman was completely different. Or so I thought. Christian knew as much as I did. We had heard of shamans but never really knew what they did or what their responsibilities were.

———

Entering Tomo's village, we were surrounded by smiling friendly children. Even though they were speaking an indian language we did not understand, we were romanced by their laughter. How could we not be?

The children took our hands and led us to a hut at the center of the village. Standing in front of the entrance was the shaman. We had heard so many stories and our expectations were exceeded by his presence. I noticed his eyes first: loving and vibrant. Christian noted how calm he was. This was a man who exuded wisdom, power, and grace.

He did not speak English so Tomo translated. I was enthralled. I wanted to sit at his feet forever. And learn. And absorb.

After a while, the shaman and Tomo's conversation became excited. We did not know what to do or what to say. Christian and I looked at each other with raised eyebrows and remained silent.

About 10 minutes later, Tomo turned to us and began to

translate. He said that he told the shaman that he was impressed with us and our love for each other, but even more for our love for Mother Amazon. In response, the shaman suggested that we might be interested to take another journey, a spiritual one. He said that it would complete the journey we had already begun.

At times, the shaman would offer visitors the opportunity to digest a certain hallucinogenic tea. This tea would open the mind, allowing it to travel through "the realms of nature and sensations of being".

What Tomo was talking about sounded to me like a trip. Like an acid trip. Like drugs. Which I did not take. Ever. I looked at Christian. He had taken drugs before and liked it. I could see from his face that he definitely wanted to drink the tea.

"Listen, babe. We will never have this experience again. Look. There is a shaman. A man. A holy man to take care of us while we trip. It will be amazing. It will make this trip unbelieveable. Unforgettable." Christian was holding my hand tight, in earnest. He really wanted me to do this.

"I don't know, honey. I am really skeptical," I said.

"You are always skeptical. You are always careful. Why not let go? We are in the Amazon Rainforest, for god's sake. Mother Amazon. You have said nothing but how amazing it all is. We have to do this. Can you imagine being one with nature more than what we already have experienced? We have to do this," he insisted.

Christian had a point. If I ever was going to try anything, it was going to be now. I had actually heard of this tea before. All I knew was that it was important not to take more than a few sips, a really small amount. Otherwise, it would be dangerous. Friends of mine had taken it when they traveled in Chile and were blown away.

Gnawing on my lip, I thought to myself. Christian was right. If I ever was going to leap to trip with Mother Nature in the Amazon. It was going to be now.

I squeezed. his hand and nodded. "Yes, let's do this. What does it taste like?"

I cannot go into the trip we took. It was surreal. As it should be. As you would expect. It was everything hallucinogenic. It was tragic. It was uplifting. It was freeing. It was catastrophic with my demons. And it challenged my angels. Drinking that tea took me on a trip beyond my imagination.

The only 'negative' part was that it lasted for three days. Three full days. But I did not know that. I had lost all concept of time. What I did know was that the journey I had started on, I must finish. I will say that the experience of those three days was earth-shattering. We fought with ourselves to free our minds, our hearts.

It was transformative for both Christian and me. As individuals and as a couple. As we slowly pulled out of the trip, I felt freer than I had ever been. I was elated from winning a war that I never knew I had been battling. Sharing my thoughts with Christian, I told him I was so happy that I had followed his lead. I leaned towards him and kissed him. I was tired, happy, in love, and free.

"I love you, baby."

Christian smiled and took me in his arms for a long hug. He felt the same and whispered his love into my ear. Releasing me from the hug, he looked into my eyes, while holding my hands and said,

"Marry me. The shaman is a holy man. Tomo told me that the shaman performs ceremonies to celebrate the union of a couple, cementing their love and honor for each other. Let's get married. What do you say?"

"You let go with me before. Now, leap with me. Marry me. Marry me here in the Amazon. Marry me with this holy man."

"Leap with me. Marry me."

And that, my friends, is how I ended up marrying Christian in a ceremony performed by a shaman of an ancient Amazon tribe, deep in the Rainforest, after coming down from a three day hallucinogenic tea trip.

It was beautiful.

I wore shorts.
So did he.
The shaman wore feathers.
I wore butterflies.
And Louie was the best man.

Lagniappe

Caipirinha

In order to be completely aligned with this story, I would ask you to drink the hallucinogenic tea which is *not* going to happen. You will, however, get to seventh heaven with *this* recipe. Because holy fricken flying monkees, is it good.

But first, caipirinhas. You cannot visit Brazil physically nor in spirit without drinking a caipirinha.

½ lime, quartered
1 teaspoon white sugar
2 ½ fluid ounces cachaca
1 cup ice cubes

1. Crush lime and sugar together.

2. Add ice and cachaca.

3. Stir. Drink. Repeat.

Acaraje Black-Eyed Pea Fritters with Shrimp Filling

40 minutes (I try to keep all my recipes short and sweet but this is worth the extra time.)

Oven: 190°C/375°F

Fritters	Filling
2 x 400g tins black-eyed peas	*1 small red onion, thinly sliced*
1 garlic clove	*1 tablespoon chopped ginger*
1 green chili, deseeded	*2 garlic cloves*
1 small red onion, diced	*1 red chili, deseeded, rough chopped*
2 tablespoon plain flour	*150g pack small raw prawns*
1 teaspoon salt	*1 tablespoon palm or vegetable oil*
1 teaspoon mild chili powder	*2 plum tomatoes, deseeded, diced*
1 teaspoon baking powder	*1 tablespoon chopped coriander*
Vegetable oil for frying	*Juice of 1 lime*
	Hot pepper sauce, to serve

1. Make the filling first. Onion, ginger, garlic, chili, and a little salt into a food processor. Purée until smooth.

2. Heat the pan with oil and fry the purée in it for 5 minutes until cooked through.

3. Add the prawns, tomatoes, and cooked coriander.

4. Squeeze in the lime and add salt to taste.

5. Cook for 3 minutes until the prawns have cooked through. Take off the stove.

———

6. Next. The fritters. Drain and rinse the black-eyed peas. Pour into a food processor and purée until smooth along with the garlic and chili.

7. Scrape into a bowl and add everything else (onion, flour, salt, chili powder, and baking powder)

8. Mix and roll into 16 balls.

———————

9. Heat pan with vegetable oil. When it is hot enough (piece of bread sizzles), drop 4 to 5 balls into the oil.

10. Fry until golden crisp which takes around 4 to 5 minutes.

11. Drain on kitchen paper while you repeat for the rest. Keep them warm in the oven.

And then — it is time to rejoice. Slice them open and add the prawn filling in. You can thank me later.

"I was an equal opportunity merchant of death. I supplied everyone but the Salvation Army...I never sold to Osama bin Laden. Not on any moral grounds: back then, he was always bouncing checks."

Andrew Niccol's Yuri Orlov in Lord of War

HOTEL CALIFORNIA
Djibouti

One day I will write an entire book about this song. Volumes of words would fill countless pages describing one memory after another, each one tied to the song: Hotel California.

Before I begin, you should know that I have never been to the original Hotel California. I think it is situated somewhere on the road to Palm Springs, south of Los Angeles.

However, I can assure you that there is more than one hotel with "mirrors on the ceiling". And there are several that host with "pink champagne on ice". And far too many where "they stab it with their steely knives but they just can't kill the beast."

I will save the digest of the many Hotel Californias around the world - for another time, dear reader.

Instead, I will tell you the story of double irony: that I sang this very song every day as my finale at a jazz bar in a "virtual" Hotel California.

To whom? An audience of arms dealers, French Legionnaires and Somali warlords.

Where? In Djibouti, a boiling outpost of salt, on the eastern horn of Africa.

———

"On a dark desert highway...."

For those of you that do not know where Djibouti is, let me help. It is a tiny country on the east coast of Africa, south of

Sudan, north of Somalia, east of Ethiopia and across the Red Sea from Yemen. It is populated by 10,000 locals, 15,000 legionnaires, 20,000 Ethiopian and Somali whores. And equally as many goats. If not more.

If you do not like goat, you are not eating. Or shrimp. There are tons of shrimp from the ocean. And that is it. There are no gardens. There are no vegetables. This is not a place where you drive up and get a kale smoothie. I do not think Arabic word for kale even exists.

However, if you want salt, this is the right place. Pepper not so much. The majority of this tiny country is covered with massive salt lakes and hundred of salt mines. Now, if only there was food to season.

How are salt lakes made? Easy answer: heat. The extreme heat that successfully evaporates water, no matter the quantity: lakes, rivers, or oceans. Which is exactly what happened here in Djibouti: what used to be lakes of water are now lakes of salt. And since the soil used to be sea bed, the salt that remains prohibits growth of any kind of vegetable. Gardens are non-existent.

Imagine living in this kind of heat, the sensation of a sunburn times 10. The heat in Djibouti is the same heat as the body temperature when you have a fever. And that is on a cool day. At high noon, the heat is so intense that it will literally melt the rubber soles of your shoes.

Not surprisingly, these temperatures define the working day, starting at 7 a.m. to finishing at 12 p.m. noon. After that, it is impossible to work. The entire country shuts down. Because nobody can function.

(By now you are thinking: air conditioning? Djibouti is one of the 10 poorest countries in the world, making electricity an obvious luxury, notwithstanding the cost of the appliances. Eating comes first. Eating is important.)

Naturally, what you wear is essential. The clothes worn by the locals are sheer, allowing air and sweat to cool the body naturally. Men wear traditional thobes, common throughout the Arabian peninsula. However it is what the women wear which makes Djibouti so interesting, given its Muslim fundamentalism. Although the dresses cover the body completely, they are made of sheer cloth and are entirely see through. Slips are worn, from hip to ankle but not so for the top, where you can see the most important part of the woman's dress: her bra. The shape of every dress is the same, but they are all different in color and design. The thin cotton material wafts with movement, following like the trail of a princess' robe, as the women walk through waves of heat. They are exotic flowers in a barren desert. This combination is unbelievably beautiful and seductive to watch.

———

"Warm smell of colitas"

When men and women are confined indoors for the most part of the day, every day, what happens? In most places, this boredom would anticipate a high appetite for drugs. But this is a Muslim country. And drugs and alcohol are outlawed.

Djibouti, however, has khat. Depending on who you talk to, khat is not a drug since chewing khat leaf has been enjoyed by locals for thousands of years. What are the effects? Imagine smoking a joint and getting a hit of coke at the same time. For men, it causes excitement and euphoria while relaxing you. However for women, chewing khat causes all of the above, with one small kick. It is the most powerful aphrodisiac in the world.

Is it popular? In Djibouti, definitely. In fact, khat is so popular that the entire country drives to the airport every day to meet the only plane that brings in khat from where it is grown in Ethiopia. The plane arrives at 2 p.m. And if it does not arrive, then the heat is not the only reason the country shuts down. Everything stops. Everything. Because everyone is frustrated, horny, and tense.

Sexual tension was apparent in closed quarters. And for this, there was service. Living in the desert with nothing to eat, and no business to make, it should be no surprise that the local women do what they can to survive. They sell themselves. Women come from all over to work. From Sudan, Ethiopia, Somalia, Eritrea, and from the salty barren plains of Djibouti. Many had travelled far for work. Because here they got it. There was a large market to service.

It was not my first time seeing those in the service industry follow the drum, but I had never seen it in so many numbers, relative to the local population. The whores outnumbered them.

You could say that the combination of khat and sex were necessities, especially if you lived in the powder keg that was Djibouti. For it is here, in Djibouti, where the warriors are trained and guns are bought. What else would be able to neutralize the lethal combination of warlords, warriors, money, and heavy religious influence on one of the poorest countries in the world, inhabited by a nation with little hope.

Djibouti is no Disneyland.

"This could be heaven or this could be hell"

Djibouti is the last garrison, the training ground for new recruits of the infamous French Legion, the veritable fight club, an army once made of criminals. More than 100 years ago, the French needed an army to police its colonies. Initially in the 1800's, it was a branch of the French Army made of foreign nationals who wanted to serve and fight. To complement the mental makeup of the Legion, "volunteers" were found in the French jails, many convicted murderers. The deal was simple: in exchange for a few years of their service, the convict would receive a new name and identity. In other words, a new life.

Highly effective, the French Legion has not only policed the colonies of France but made a few as well, primarily throughout Africa. Countries and continents have been formed under the auspice of the military execution of the Foreign Legion. Since then, the French Legion has expanded and accepted applications from all nationalities. Members come from more than 140 countries now. If accepted, the tradition continues: with the compulsory five years served, the soldier would receive a new identity with a French passport. Only the best of humanity need apply.

Make no mistake. This is the most lethal battalion on the planet. They are exceptional. Five years in the French Legion is not boot camp in the park. You are psychologically and physically broken down before they build you up again into a fighting machine. The French Legion are the fiercest warriors, with an incompatible esprit de corps, a loyalty and allegiance only to the Legion. (Not to France, only to the Legion. Interestingly enough.)

The new recruits would arrive in Djibouti and be immediately placed in barracks. Full sun. No shade. For weeks. Very few last beyond two weeks. During this time, extreme physical activity is demanded while water withheld. Some survive and some do not. You might think that barracks in the sun is not that big of a deal; however, if the sun is hot enough to melt rubber, it would melt your resistance, too. Making an army out of criminals that jails cannot handle is not an easy task, but the French do it. Discipline is enforced at all times, covering every aspect of their life on the field of battle and off. All this before they even start training you to be a warrior.

And that is only two weeks in, imagine 5 years.

"Stab it with their steely knives, but they just can't kill the beast..."

At the time of this story, peace was the official reason for Somali warlords to come to Djibouti. For more than 40 years, generations of warlords had run the former Italian colony. Pockets of insurgents were now gaining strength, primarily those infused by religious faith. There were many players keeping war alive, and far too few coming to the table to discuss detente. Sustaining war is not cheap. By any standard.

War is never just about religion. The economic potential of

Somalia: besides the richness of land and fish (to feed the entire eastern coast of Africa) and an abundance of mining capabilities (diamonds, coltan ore), Somalia has the largest offshore oil reserves in the world. The kind that would alter the oil powerhouse of Saudi Arabia and completely change the landscape of OPEC.

Some may call it a naive or romantic hope that the Somali warlords were in Djibouti to discuss peace other than raising war chests, negotiating funds, or buying arms. I always heralded those who chose to cling and chase the ghost of peace. It was my hope that maybe the people of Somalia and their leaders were tired of war. That there had been too much killing and they had seen too much blood.

History written since those days has proven otherwise. Sometimes a baptism of blood can never be reversed. Peace is forever elusive. The dead do not have names or numbers on a page. The babies born today are children dead tomorrow. If they are lucky enough to survive, they become fighters themselves, aging into warlords that later come to Djibouti to negotiate peace, while they chew khat and drink tea with the French warriors trained to enforce it.

"Plenty of room at the Hotel California"

There is really only one hotel in Djibouti. There was one hotel for guests. There was only one hotel for restaurants. There was only one hotel that had a bar. There was only one hotel that had a dance floor.

And this one hotel had a hotel lobby where everyone who was anyone would come to discuss business during the 'off hours' of the day. Ergo, it was full by 12.30 and packed after the plane came in at 2 p.m.

The lobby was the safe space, a "Switzerland" for all types of discussions between warlords, legionnaires, arms dealers, UN officials, and locals alike. It was little piece of civilization in a desert of morality.

These people were my audience. Every day at 3 p.m., I would sing with the residential jazz band.

I actually only meant to sing once. One day, I had finished work early and was sitting in the lobby, drinking mint tea, listening to the music. The hotel was empty as it habitually was for the half hour to go and come back from the airport. Usually, I would just hum to myself. But that one day, they started to play my song. And I went up to the microphone and started singing. I had to.

Apparently, it was a hit. I was asked to sing again the following day. The following day. And the day after that. Each time my audience grew.

For the duration of my time there, I would sing a compilation of songs, covering the greats from Ella to Etta. All jazz. With one exception: my finale, Hotel California. It was a must. It was my song. It had become an anthem, a soundtrack, lyrics for a headstone, descriptive in their insanity:

"You can come any time you like, but you can never leave."

====

Lagniappe

There are two dishes eaten every day in Djibouti: shrimp cocktail and goat kebab. However, given that goat is not "common" outside of Djibouti, I will share with you the recipe for a classic shrimp cocktail.

You can never go wrong with a shrimp cocktail. Or any cocktail, for that matter...

Shrimp Cocktail
10 minutes

Fast and Dirty Cocktail Sauce
½ cup ketchup
2 tablespoons horseradish
Worcestershire sauce
1 lemon
Season: salt, pepper, tabasco sauce

1. Combine all and chill.

Classic Easy Shrimp
10 cups water
1 lemon
2 bay leaves
15 whole peppercorns
15 to 20 raw shrimp, deveined and peeled with tails left on them

1. Boil the water with lemon, bay leaves and peppercorns.
2. Add the shrimp until they are pink.
3. Take the shrimp out and place them into an ice bath. (This will stop them cooking.)

Serve with cocktail sauce and (of course) a cocktail.

"Your soulmate will be the stranger you recognize."

Unknown

SLIDING DOORS OF SERENDIPITY
United Kingdom

"Hurry up!" Claire was yelling back at me, as she ran across the street. The double decker bus was about to pass us but had slowed for the stop lights.

"I am coming!" I was running behind her. She was going fast. That being said, she was not the one carrying the huge bag.

I was.

"Run faster! We need to catch that bus." I really do not know how people can run and talk at the same time. It is beyond me. I have enough trouble running and breathing simultaneously. Having a conversation is downright difficult.

But she was right and this was no joke. We needed to catch the bus. The next one was in 30 minutes. Now, when you have 30 minutes free and you are living in the Bahamas, congratulations. You live a life that I do not. 30 minutes in the sun and warm weather is slightly different than 30 minutes in the rain and cold.

Nobody has ever called London a tropical hotspot.

Ever.

Running full speed ahead and determined, Claire was in place and in time to catch the bus. She started begging the driver to wait the few seconds, (ok, 60 of them) until I could reach them. She is a star. Claire, that is. The bus driver was not so happy, but I was ever so grateful that he had waited.

"Thank you, thank you!" I do not know if he understood me through my out-of-breath wheezing. To add to the stress, my bus money was of course on the bottom of my bag. (My bag is actually a suitcase since I was moving back home from China.)

After a few silent curses and audible apologies to the passengers on the bus, I found my purse and paid the gentleman bus driver. Whew.

All eyes were on us. We were the delinquents that had stopped the bus for 30 extra seconds.

I blushed from the attention, turning my face more scarlet rose than English rose. Combine the look with being drenched, sopping wet hair, and one could say that I was the furthest pick from anyone's choice for fashion magazine cover girl.

Hey ho. I was not going to meet the man of my dreams here anyway.

What drama. Weaving through the people, Claire and I started looking for a place to sit as the doors closed and the bus continued on its route.

Now, so far this is a perfectly normal story. One that happens every day. People catch buses. They run after them. No matter where they are in the world. In the sun. In the rain. In fact, more people miss buses than there are actual buses. I would put money on it that I think everyone in their lifetime has missed a bus.

But this time it was different. This time I not only caught the bus.

"Putain, merde."

Are you serious? Shit. We just missed the bus. I looked at my friend, Henri, with disappointment. We were going to be late. Really late.

We had sprinted after the bus. Literally sprinted. I am tall enough that my sprints are more like a gallop, and still the bus did not stop. Correction: would not stop. I was hitting the door as it pulled away.

"Stop!" I demanded, but the bus driver ignored me and turned his face away as he pulled into the traffic. No eye contact whatsoever.

"Putana Eva!" Curse words tripled over themselves in every language I knew. All directed at the bus driver, the razor that cut my face while shaving, the coffee maker that broke this morning, the iron that burned the back of my shirt. I was cursing at everything. It was a bad day. And it had just started.

And now this. The bus that would not stop. I watched it drive away.

Away from home. Away from me. The icing on the cake was that it was raining. Not the gentle rain that floats over soft pastures. But the London rain that slaps you across the face, tearing umbrellas to pieces.

Lovely. Not.

I was soaked. We both were. Henri was cursing. His umbrella had succumbed to the elements and now he was as drenched as I was. Abandoned and in the middle of a downpour.

Damnit.

So much for the iron. I did not need that anymore. Wet shirts wrinkle. What I needed was an umbrella. Which of course I forgot as I had run out of the house. Looking around, Henri and I saw a shelter from the rain, a makeshift bus stop. Steaming curses, we walked (more like stomping) to our waiting post and tried to huddle underneath the small shelter. Which is not easy for two grown men, both taller than 6 feet.

This was so not cool.

Suck. The next bus would be in 30 minutes. We were going to have to wait 30 minutes. In the cold. In the rain.

England. I could not wait to leave here. This grey. This weather. So different from my home of Italy. But I should not complain. The buses actually show up here. I do not remember the last time I saw a bus in Puglia.

Now that I was completely late, I needed to get to a phone to make arrangements, but did not see any phone booths around. "Dios, no!" I was really stuck. This was not going to look good. First day on the job and I am late. That being said, it was only training day. I might be able to get away with it. The job really started tomorrow when I left for my first posting in Romania.

I could not wait. It was the adventure of a lifetime. A beautiful city and a great team. The job was fascinating. I loved being a journalist and after a lot of work, I finally got my first foreign posting. Romania. It is not a war zone. But welcome nonetheless. And I was packed and ready to go.

It might be cold there. But at least I would be out of the rain.

A couple of jokes and a few cigarettes later, our mood had lightened. Then I saw the red color of the double decker bus weaving its way towards us. Finally.

The tension in my stomach eased as I started to exhale. I really hated being late. Don't get me wrong. I am not saint when it comes to time. It is part of my DNA. There is fashionably late, Italian late, and very late. But today, I was very very late.

The bus slowed to a stop and we boarded. I had been holding onto the money for the past 30 minutes. We paid quickly and the doors closed behind us before taking off again.

The bus was crowded. Jam packed. There was a small standing space in the middle of the bus. It was right next to a girl crouched over her bag. She was mumbling to herself. The girl looked as wet as I was, so I did not think it would matter if I dripped on her. Being tall and soaking wet in a crowded bus, I was sure that whoever bumped into me was not going to be dry. Tough, I thought to myself. This was England. It was always raining and I was tall. What am I supposed to do?

She finished packing away her things, and dragging her hand through her hair, out of her face, she started to stand, "Claire, you know what?" And looked at me.

I looked back.

"Why, hello," she said.

"Hello" I replied. Stunned. Wow. She is gorgeous. My brain stopped. "Hello" was the only word I could think of. Kicking myself into action, I should try smiling.

Which I did. Then she smiled back. She was already beautiful and now she transformed into an angel. Suddenly, I was thanking god for making me miss the bus. Because I would have missed this. I would have missed her. Grazie Dio. Thank you Lord. Merci Dieu.

"Ciao." I really could not think of anything else. I needed to get it together. Henri kicked me. He could see what was going on. Shaking my head, I turned back to the girl.

"My name is Marc. Yours?" I asked.

"Caroline," she answered and stretched out her hand. I took it and leaned over to give her a kiss on the cheek.

"Nice to meet you," she continued.
"Nice to meet you, too," I answered.

How long did I have on this bus with her? Could anyone make the bus slow down?

———

Of course now would be the time that I would meet the most gorgeous man I had ever seen. Of course, Murphy's law. Wet, dirty, running make up, red faced, and tired. I literally could not have tried to look worse. But of course, this would be the time when a Roman god appears. Dripping wet but still godlike.

He said something to me. It must be his name. I stuck out my hand and introduced myself. It seemed completely normal, except for my beating heart. Who is this man and why is he kissing me? Why is he leaning in? Ah, he is European. A kiss on the cheek. Nice.

I smiled. It was nice to meet him. And I said so. He looked confused and then he smiled. "Nice to meet you, too."

Thank God, I caught this bus. Or rather, thank you, Claire. I looked over to her. She was smiling. She knew what was going on. I was blushing and this man was delicious.

How long was this bus ride? I was all of a sudden thankful that London transport was so slow. Because, I was no longer in any rush.

———

We talked the entire hour the bus took to get into town. It was as if she was the only passenger on the bus. Only us. Henri tried to make eye contact with Claire but I payed him no mind. I was fully focused on her.

"Have coffee with me? Or better yet, have dinner with me tonight. I leave tomorrow but have dinner with me tonight?" I asked her as we pulled into Charing Cross Station, holding my breath for her answer.

She paused. She looked down at her bag. She looked at Claire. She looked at me. "Yes." She said yes.

I exhaled and smiled again.

———

What did I just say yes to?
Of course, I said yes.
I said yes to dinner that night.
And to the kiss later that evening.
And yes to keeping in touch.
And then yes again to flying to visit him in Romania.
And then yes again to flying to see him at his next posting.
And then yes to meeting him in Rome.

And then yes to travelling with him to Hong Kong.
And then yes to meeting him in Ghana.
And yes to the posting after that in California.
And then yes to joining him in Nigeria.
And then yes to working with him in London.
And yes to living with him.
And yes to marrying him.
And yes to having two boys with him.
And yes to living 19 years with him.

Just yes.

Simple, no?

Just like catching a bus.

━━━━━━━━

─────

P.S. When they told me this story the first time, I thought this was real life "Sliding Doors" but better. Because it actually happened. I love their story. I am in awe of it. It is true love at first sight. One for the ages. They are magic. Still almost 20 years later.

You should know one thing though: since the day they told me that story, I never miss a bus. Ever.

Lagniappe

If you do nothing else, drink rose champagne while you read this story. It is a love story after all.

But if you are hungry for something quintessentially British, try the London broil. It is easy. It is good. And it has London in the title. Job done. It will take you 5 minutes to prepare and 5 minutes to grill. Serve with a pint of dark ale or red wine. Some people also like vegetables, like mushy peas and mashed potatoes. Whatever takes your fancy.

London Broil
Time: 4 hours total

2 pounds London Broil Beef
2 tablespoons Worcestershire sauce
¼ cup balsamic vinegar
¼ soy sauce
¼ cup olive oil
2 garlic cloves
1 teaspoon rosemary
¼ teaspoon pepper

Note: I add red wine, pomegranate seeds, mustard. I just throw everything in. Including the kitchen sink.

1. Put it all in a bag, ziploc and let sit for 3 to 4 hours. If overnight, then make sure to take out the meat 30 minutes before you cook it so that the meat starts cooking already at room temperature.

2. Broil for 5 to 7 minutes on each side. Or grill 10 minutes on each side.

Really, it is that easy.

Done. Now for the pint…

"Seas the day."

Unknown

Surfing Hippos

Kenya

It was a beautiful day in Naivasha. A perfect day for windsurfing. I could feel it in my bones, sensing it in the way the air touched my skin. The wind gods were happy.

Finishing my morning coffee, I grabbed my board, put it in the back of my truck and drove down to the beach. Eager. I could not wait to get in the water.

Setting up quickly, I was off. The sun was shining, the wind was at my back, and it was glorious. I was flying over the waves, fast.

And then all of a sudden, I abruptly came to a grinding halt. Which is perfectly acceptable when you have beached. But when you are in the middle of the water? That never happens. It is impossible.

I was well aware of the sand dunes, having sussed them out on previous rides. Nothing is a greater buzz killer when you are whipping through the waves and then - boom! - fall because the board beached on a sand dune.

So, knowing I beached far from any dune and far from the shore, you could say I was a bit concerned. Maybe more than a bit.

And that tiny amount of concern grew into full blown WTF when I started going upward. Just in case, you missed that: I was going up. Direction up. Not the direction 'forward' which is what happens when you are on a board with the wind at your back.

I was beached. And I was going up. Very strange, wouldn't you agree?

No stranger than the heart attack of my reality: I had beached on top of a hippo's back.

Yes, people. I was going up.
On my surfboard.
Because I had beached on top of a hippo.

Hippo.

Perfectly normal.

Not.

———

Harry the Hippo, (of course I named him) was certainly as alarmed as I was.
Of course, it is not every day that Harry would have a heavy board and a grown man come to a grinding halt on his back.

Harry did seem a bit perturbed. More like angrily stunned. He was blowing water through his nose, like a submarine surfacing. For those of you who do not know what hippos look like, let me offer you a quick explanation: they are huge. Huge.

Huge like a hippo.

They also happen to be the fiercest animals on the safari.

Making the obvious split second decision, I ditched the surfboard and took off in a running sprint, only to fall into the water with a huge splash. Quickly kicking my feet to surface, I swam as fast as I could to get away from Harry...

Thank god hippos are not as fast as sharks. Their girth prohibits them from pivoting and taking off after their prey. They only eat prey served to them on a platter.

Like me.

I made it safely to the beach, unscathed. It took a few minutes for the heart to slow down. Holy macro.

Holy hippo.

Speaking of which, Harry had turned his rage to the surfboard. Yeah, the board was gone.

But that was ok. I considered it a fair exchange.

Harry got the board.

And I got the story.

Over the past few years, I have taught hundreds of people to swim, to dive, to surf: body, wind, and kite. It is my passion. It is my calling.

I could wax poetic about being in the water. Swimming in the ocean, the sea or in the pool, I feel as if I have come home. Whereas being on land always feels foreign to me. Water is my holy grail. I am proud to be a full fledged member of every single water sport imaginable, a veritable water puppy.

Especially when it comes to surfing. There is nothing like harnessing the wind to send you skirting over the waves, the feeling of speed, combined with being one with the elements, is a the highest natural high that everyone should experience at least once in his lifetime.

Not all my clients or students love the water. Some fear the water as they do taking a plane. Some abhor spiders. Others fear snakes. Some will never bungee jump. Others have a fear of heights.

Most of those who have a fear of the water are usually because: one, they cannot swim, or two, they have seen a scary movie about what lies beneath the ocean's surface. Interestingly enough, children are rarely scared of water. In fact, up to the age of 6 months, they can swim without prior instruction and hold their breath with ease. (Do not try this at home.) Something, somewhere along the way alters the way that baby feels about water later on.

Respecting that, the first thing I do as an instructor is to listen and talk extensively with my students. I have found that personifying water works very well. Talking to our natural curiosity, information will usually leads us, quite literally, to the water's edge.

I describe elements of biology and how our bodies are made to spend extensive amounts of time in the water. For instance, how our body naturally protects the heart, reversing the flow of oxygen to the heart while underwater. Or that while in the water, our hands naturally become shriveled, enabling us to pick up things.

Water is a natural habitat for us. As it is for many other animals. When we are on dry land, we do not pay much attention to the other creatures we share the planet with, like the birds and bees. We respect that we share the same home. We don't take the nests out of the trees nor do we disrupt a bee hive. We should behave the same underwater.

The only difference is the way we breathe. There is so much to explore, to discover, to enjoy. It is the playground for all and home for many animals on this planet. Including hippos.

And every once in awhile, I share a few of my own stories before introducing my students to the pool. Guess which story I start with?

"Once upon a time, there was a hippo called Harry...."

Lagniappe

I am partial to beer when I surf but I must admit I do like a gin and tonic every once in a while. Especially while on safari.

When you get hungry, try this recipe for Githeri, a homegrown favorite of all Kenyans. It might take some time, but it definitely is comfort food, and filling. Probably because it has everything in it.

Githeri
45 minutes

2 cups dry mixed beans
2 cups corn
250 gram steak, cut into cubes
1 cube of beef stock
2 tablespoons oil
1 onion, chopped
2 tomatoes, chopped
2 potatoes, boiled, peeled and chopped
2 green chilies, chopped
1 tablespoon tomato paste
1 tablespoon garlic paste
½ teaspoon cumin powder
¼ red chili powder
¼ tumeric powder
1 lemon, juiced
Season: ginger, garlic salt and pepper

1. Boil and cook beans and corn until tender. Drain and put aside. Save the water for later.
2. Boil the steak until tender in water which has ¼ teaspoon of salt, pepper, ginger, and garlic.
3. Heat onion in pan until transparent, adding tomato paste and garlic paste

4. Add tomatoes.

5. Cook on low heat, stirring to make sure it does not stick to the bottom of the pan.

6. Add chilies, meat, and beans.

7. Mix, stir with water from the meat or beef stock cube. Season with salt and pepper.

8. Simmer over low heat until flavors combine to taste. Add lemon juice to taste.

Serve with extra chilies or lemon.

After a hearty bowl, you will not be moving. Settle in for the night.

BONUS

This recipe does not scream Kenyan local authenticity, but I will say I had this for the first time on safari, and then again at a friend's house at Lake Naivasha, and I asked for it again when I went back on safari. So that counts. Right? You will see. It is so damn good.

Bacon Wrapped BBQ Chicken Lollipops
45 minutes

10 chicken legs
10 strips bacon
1 teaspoon salt
1 teaspoon soy sauce
½ teaspoon red chili paste
1 teaspoon white vinegar
1 teaspoon green chili, chopped
1 teaspoon celery, chopped
1 tablespoon spring onions, chopped
4 tablespoons wheat flour

1. Combine soy sauce, red chili paste, vinegar, garlic, celery, spring onions, and green chilies: Mix well.
2. Push the meat down on each chicken leg. Add to mixture and marinate for 30 minutes.
3. Remove chicken legs from the marinade and add flour to make a batter.
4. Wrap the legs in bacon.
5. Dip the chicken legs in batter
6. Grill for 30 minutes on medium heat, turning every 5 minutes, until done.

You can thank me later.

"Each contact with a human being is so rare, so precious, one should preserve it."

Anais Nin

A LIFETIME OF FLOWERS

Philippines

There is nothing like riding in the front seat of a car. I personally love it. You can roll down the window and let the breeze in. Better yet, rest your arm on the side of the car and feel the wind flow through your fingers. And let's not forget about the music. The perfect complement to a breeze is a rocking tune on the radio. All the senses are activated when you are being driven. The windshield is your movie screen. And when you are in the city, the sounds of traffic and busy life give a surround sound, layering the intensity.

When travelling in a taxi, I always sit in the front. I love the movie as it turns to the unfamiliar, transported through time and culture, soaking in the sounds and the smells of the foreign land.

One evening while living in Manila, I was in a taxi with a few friends, on our way to the opening of a new restaurant. We were looking forward to a weekend of indulgence, washing away the stress of the days before.

Tapping my hand to the music while feeling the sensation of the breeze, I was thoroughly enjoying my 'movie': the live 3D technicolor movie of Manila by night, complete with the honks and horns of the surrounding cars, so loud that it competed with the sounds of our laughter.

I loved it.

We pulled up to a red light and stopped in traffic, massive since the customary two lanes now held four lanes of cars. It was in the middle of all this - the throng, the noise, the laughter - that my 'movie' stopped and my attention went to someone outside the car touching my arm.

It was a little flower girl, common to street corners in Manila during the day. This one had braved the traffic and the night to sell me a necklace of flowers. Not more than 7 or 8 years old, she was tiny, with long brown hair, big brown eyes, in tattered clothes. She looked like hundreds of other kids in Manila, all selling flowered necklaces, trying to make a living, one car at a time.

From early in the morning to late at night, I was asked to buy flower necklaces. So, why was this time so different? I was used to poverty. Or so I thought, after living for one year in Cuba. But it this particular encounter changed my life.

There was me, in a new suit, in a taxi, driving to an expensive restaurant for a night out on the town, while she was clothed in a dress that ten other people had worn before her. Her daily diet of food was probably rice.

Feeling the twinge of guilt, I reached into my pocket and gave her money to buy a necklace. It was probably around the equivalent of $25, way over the price of 25 cents. I wanted to give it to her, believing it would help her in a small way. It was not a life-changer, but it was at least something.

Stunned, the little girl looked at the wad of cash in one hand and the flowers in another. She looked at me. She looked at her hands. And then panic began to form on her face. With terror in her eyes, she looked at me and then back behind her.

This was not what I was expecting. Where did the terror come from? I thought I might see gratitude, but not terror.

She thrust the flowers at me. Of course, I rejected them. I wanted her to have the flowers to sell. All night long or perhaps for tomorrow. The money was a gift, a donation. I would take one necklace but certainly not all of them. The others necklaces she could sell, adding to her bonus at the end of the night.

Or so I thought.

Looking back on the entire sequence of the memory, what I remember most is the look of panic on her face. To this day, I clearly remember her eyes: the fear on the face of an angel. I did not understand then, why the terror, why she felt that way, why she kept on insisting that I take the flowers.

I continued to reject them. And she continued to push them towards me. I did not speak Tagalog, so the entire exchange was in sign language. Finally, after what looked like a split second of internal processing, the moment changed. The look of panic became one of determination. She thrust all the flowers onto my lap, over the edge of the window of the taxi, and took off running down the lanes of the ghetto into the busy backstreets of Manila.

The honking of the cars behind us had now reached an ear-piercing volume, forcing us to leave the scene. With my lap full of flowers, we drove on, silent in reflection of what had just occurred.

Now you might ask, what is so special about this story? The poor little girl gave all her flowers in exchange for money. On the surface, that would seem the case. But we are only looking at the surface. What makes this particular story poignant is the why.

Why did she do that, when she could have earned more by selling the other necklaces? I kept on thinking about this throughout the night. I did not understand as to why she would give up the opportunity to make more money.

And then it dawned on me. It was not about the money. It was not about how much I gave her nor how much she could earn. I could have given her $50 or $100 - it would not have changed a thing.

For what she valued was time. Not money. She had no money. She lived surrounded by no money. She knew the value of money, needing to beg for it day in and day out. Night after night. Car after car. And although knowing how money could affect her life immediately - she, with nothing, chose to spend time on herself instead.

Perhaps she chose time because she knew that time is needed for an education. Perhaps she chose time because she wanted to play, like a girl should at her age. Perhaps she chose time to invest in herself in another way, knowing that cute street urchins do not stay cute forever. They grow up, and if not prepared, will walk the streets, selling different wares altogether.

I do not know what she decided to do with her time when she ran down the street. I did not follow her. The interaction was short, intense, abrupt. What I do know is that she who had nothing and had to beg every day, decided to sacrifice money in exchange for something that we all have. Time.

If the little flower girl, a street urchin, valued time over money, shouldn't I do the same?

———————

Lagniappe

This dish is famous throughout the Philippines. And rightly so. Whatever you decide to drink with this dish, make it cold. It is hot and humid in the Philippines.

Chicken Adobo
50 minutes

6 boned, skinless chicken thighs
3 cloves garlic
⅔ apple cider vinegar
⅓ cup soy sauce
1 tablespoon whole black peppercorns
1 bay leaf
1 tablespoon vegetable oil

1. Brown the chicken on both sides on medium high heat. 5 minutes on each side before removing the chicken from the pan.

2. In the same pan, complete with drippings, add the rest of the ingredients. When they are soft (garlic), return the chicken to the pan. Use the sauce to coat the chicken.

3. Cook, covered for 20 minutes. Continue spooning the chicken with the sauce.

4. Uncover the chicken, decrease the heat to medium low, and cook for another 15 minutes. The sauce will thicken. The chicken will be glazed with sauce. Beautiful.

It is ready now. Enjoy with rice.

PS. Sometimes, the locals add coconut milk. And use pork instead of chicken. There are always options for something so delicious.

Ube Ice Cream

7 hours

The Philippines has magnificent food; the cuisine is to die for. I love this recipe because of the taste and color. Seriously, what is better than purple ice cream?

2½ cups cream
1½ cup milk
1¼ cups sugar
4 eggs yolks, lightly beaten
2 cups cooked mashed ube (purple yam)
1 tsp vanilla extract
Drops of red food color and blue food color

1. In a saucepan, combine cream, milk and sugar. Heat slowly while continuously mixing until it reaches nearly boiling point (do not boil) and sugar is completely dissolved.

2. Place egg yolks into a mixing bowl then slowly pour around a cup of the heated cream mixture while whisking.

3. Pour egg mixture into the saucepan. Continue to heat while continuously mixing. Dip a tablespoon and see if liquid sticks to the back side; if it does then you can now turn the heat off.

4. Place in a heat proof container; add drops of red food colour and blue food colour, continue adding until desired colour is achieved. Purple!

5. Add vanilla extract then let it cool in the fridge for at least four hours.

6. Pour the cream mixture together with mashed ube into the ice cream maker and churn for 30-35 minutes.

You can now eat the ice cream at this stage, but if you want it harder, then let it freeze for at least 6 hours.

"To live…to live would be an awfully big adventure."

Peter Pan

THE KING AND I, A FAIRYTALE

Gulf States

Not everybody gets to have tea with a King in the Middle East.

Especially after you have been deported.

Normally, that would be considered illegal. And definitely would not be permitted. If you are barred from being in the country, you would definitely not be allowed in the presence of the King. But this was more than a fairytale. This was real life. This happened.

Sometimes, Alladin's Genie is not just a fable, and sometimes, the Fairy Godmother does not work only for Cinderella. And sometimes, happy endings happen in the 21st century.

———

To start off, the happy ending is me not being killed. I was already in love and recently married. My prince had come. Before I knew it, he had whisked me away on a magic carpet, off to foreign lands, a small country in the Gulf.

After a few months of lying by the pool, (call it an extended honeymoon), I got bored. And started looking for a job. There were not many jobs in general. And even fewer if you were not a local. The pickings were slim. The very few positions available for women were often in retail. Call it magic, because before long I had a job, selling prêt a porter.

I was lucky with the job but not so lucky with my boss. She was the spawn child of the Wicked Witch of the West and the Evil Stepmother. If that was possible. This woman wasn't just awful. She was heinously manipulative.

There was nothing I could do about it. Her father was "Jafar", so she was untouchable, like having an evil magic spell protecting her.

I asked her one day why she treated me so badly. She just smiled at me and then smiled at my husband. I swear I saw her fangs drop while she licked her lips.

Oh no, honey. Not on my watch. That was never happening. Never never land was that ever happening. That man was mine. She could turn herself into Tinker Bell for all I cared. She could try and weave her magic, with dresses cut down to there and feathers in her hair. But this man was mine. Repeat after me. My man. My Peter.

(By the way, in case you were wondering, my name is Wendy. For realz.)

And so a cold war ensued between me (Wendy) and Tinker Twit (my new name for her). We were cordial but lethal to each other. Let me rephrase: I was cordial and she was lethal.

You see, she could not get rid of me either. My protective Fairy Godmother was in the form of the young Prince of the kingdom. Besides Tinker's want for money and prestige, what drove her crazy was that I not only had the most amazing husband in the world, but the young Prince saw me as his older sister.

(Princess Wendy. I could get down with that. It has a nice ring to it.)

He would come by the shop every couple of days to sit and chit chat. He would talk about girls, and then he would talk about boys, confused as every teenager is. Which was only compounded with the responsibility awaiting him on the horizon. With me, he was relaxed. With me, he had a friend.

But this friendship was not acceptable in Tinker Twit's book. Oh no. Evil spells were made and words of venom were dropped on the lap of the Immigration Office(r).

So, one afternoon on my day off, I was informed by the Immigration Office(r) that I had a couple of hours to pack my bags before I would be escorted to the airport and put on the next flight out.

"What! This will not stand!" I told him as I slammed the phone down. I was angry. I was furious. Most of all, I was not going to be separated from my husband, escorted out of the country like a criminal. I was completely innocent. Completely.

Rushing, I drove to the shop in order to speak face to face with the Prince. Since it was not allowed to drop in on him at the palace, I would have to wait until he passed by the shop on his daily walk through the mall. Even if I tried reaching him on his phone, he had a protective entourage. I was not sure I would speak to him on time.

Waiting for him to pass by was probably the longest two hours of my life. Each minute felt like an hour. I was wishing, hoping, praying, worried, but most of all, I was angry.

Oh brother, I was angry. Tinker Twit was not winning this fight.

Welcome to Wendy's World. My manicured hands leave marks. The challenge would not go unanswered.

———

Fairytales do have happy endings. This is what happened next: the young Prince turned into my Fairy Godmother. He waved his hand and the decree for my deportation was struck from the books. In Tipp-Ex I believe. Or a snap of his fingers. Either or. Both worked.

The only stipulation was that I would not work at the store. Not a problem. I happily back went back to being in honeymoon mode, spending most of my time tanning by the pool along with the occasional modeling job. Life was tough but somebody had to do it.

It was there by the pool where I met a group of ladies,

stewardesses by day, the King's mistresses by night. They were not only beautiful but fascinating and kind, worthy of an Aladdin's fortune.

Which is what they got paid for their time. One afternoon, after a few drinks by the pool, I was invited to Sheryl's apartment. She wanted to show me her treasure chest, because that is exactly what it was: gems of every color, ropes of pearls, necklaces of diamonds, rubies, and sapphires. A treasure chest. A fortune. One that could make a King. One that was given by a king.

He doted on her. In fact, I think he loved her. The King would hold fabulous parties for her, just to make her happy. My husband and I were invited to one on the beach. I was so excited; I was going to meet the King. What do I say? How should I behave? I had no idea. I had never received any indication of royal protocol.

Sheryl told me. The rules were simple:
Do not do anything until the King does it first.
Do not eat before he does.
Do not sit before he invites you.

It seemed easy enough for me. Follow the leader. Now the next question was - the most important question was - what do I wear? When I asked, she winked, "A bikini, darling. We will be at the beach."

Ok then. Nothing like meeting the King of a Gulf State in a bikini for cocktails. I like this kind of protocol.

Upon arrival, the first thing I noticed were the women in bikinis, dancing along the water. Higher up on the beach was a massive tent with carpets, couches, candles, chandeliers, and countless tables of food. There was live music in the background. Much to the enjoyment of onlookers, some of the girls were belly dancing to the music.

The King was center stage, happily reclining on a plush satin couch, surrounded by his entourage, watching the entertainment while being fed by Sheryl.

Calling us over, he greeted us warmly and invited us to sit down and join him for tea and cake. Places were made ready, pillows were fluffed, and dishes prepared for us at the table. We sat next to the Prince. It was so lovely to see him again. I had not seen my Fairy Godmother since he had saved the day (and my life). It was good to be with him, sharing stories, and to hear how he was doing. I had missed him and his friendship.

It was a wonderful afternoon, above and beyond anything I could have dreamed of. It was Cinderella's ball in the sand.

And then Tinker came into the tent. The look of astonishment on her face was priceless. She had expected me to be gone, deported, away forever. She did not expect to see me laughing with the King and the Prince. This was the company that she could only dream of keeping and the influence that she would never have.

And there I was laughing. Eating cake. With the King. Speaking with the Prince. In love and married to Peter.

Living happily ever after.

———————

Lagniappe

Adeni Tea is probably my favorite tea, especially when made the right way. It is delicious. Simply divine. It is dessert in a tea. Who can ask for more?

PS. I always ask for more...and in this case, you must join me and have a piece of cake. Any kind. Your choice. If you can't make up your mind, have chocolate.

Adeni Tea
10 minutes

3 cups water
2 tea bags
6 ounces of evaporated milk
5 to 10 cardamom pods, crushed
3 to 4 whole cloves
¼ ground cinnamon
⅛ nutmeg
Honey to taste

1. Over medium heat, boil everything, except the tea, for 8 to 10 minutes until you can smell the spices.
2. Add the tea and let cook for a couple of minutes until the tea turns the color that you like.

Make lots of it because one glass will not be enough.

"Oh, it's such a perfect
day. I'm glad I spent
it with you."

Lou Reed

DITCHING TRAINS
Belgium & Holland

When I woke up this morning, I had no idea I would be negotiating in sign language with a prostitute sitting on the other side of a glass window. I didn't think I was going to be in Amsterdam. I don't even live in Holland.

And yet, here I was in the red light district of Amsterdam, signing with a prostitute because I was curious about the street value of blow jobs.

For academic reasons, of course. It's kind of like the price of a Big Mac is an economic indicator, changing from country to country. It must be the same for blow jobs, right? Same, same but different.

Actually, I was really asking her if we could use her room to sleep. We needed a bed. Would she rent out her bed? Every single other room in Amsterdam was occupied. At least those rooms in our price range: we were penniless students, who had already spent all our money on beer.

Thinking that it would help persuade her in our favor, I gestured that as a matter of respect for her profession, we would wear ear plugs. However, I do not think she tracked with me very well. Jumping from signing the price for a blow job, to signing that we would wear earplugs while she worked, would be a leap for anyone.

Standing next to me was Scott. Who was in shock. To be fair, I am not certain what he was thinking, but I am pretty sure that he did not think this was romantic. Or anywhere close to anyone's idea of romance. His itinerary for a successful date did not include having the girl negotiate with a prostitute in Amsterdam.

Bring girl to Amsterdam: A+
Party all day: A+
Not find bed: D
Have girl negotiate the price of a blow job with prostitutes: F

Where does a guy go from there?
Yes, really where did he go from there?

––––––––––

"I have an idea. Do you want to go check out towns outside of Brussels on Saturday? You know, see a bit of Belgium?" Scott asked me after class one day.

"Sure. I'm up for an adventure. Why not? You got any ideas?" I replied.

Scott and I were in a study group together. We had gravitated to each other in class as he was one of the few Americans who went to our university. It was good to have a fellow American as a friend.

"Yeah, I have an idea. Just meet me around 11 a.m. at the Central Station."

"Cool," I thought. My first year at school in Brussels and with so much going on, I had not really been able to explore.

Saturday quickly came around. And I was at the station ready to go, waiting for him at the meeting point. Scott walked up to me with two tickets in his hand. He was smiling at me, as if he had this super secret.

"What's up? What's going on?" I had spider sense. Something was off.

"Nothing. Just come with me." Scott answered and took my elbow to follow him. We walked to the platform and got on the train. The sign read "Antwerp" on the side of the train.

Cool, I thought. I had only briefly visited Antwerp once before. It would be great to go back.

Finding seats, we got situated and comfortable. Scott reached into his backpack and took out a bottle of wine and two glasses.

The penny dropped. This was a date. Oh shit. I did not think this was a date.

(I have always been stupid about these things. I never understand what is going on; I just don't pick up the signals. For the record, I still don't. Age has taught me nothing.)

And, it seemed we were not going to Antwerp.

Pouring a glass of wine, Scott looked at me and asked,

"Ever been to Amsterdam?"

———————

I drank it.

The glass.

And then the bottle.

By the time we arrived in Amsterdam, we were downright tipsy, and the initial anxiety had worn off. I was ready for a day of exploration, walking the streets of Amsterdam, checking out the museums, eating at a cheap restaurant, and a having a few beers before heading home. Great day, right? What could go wrong?

(I was determined it was going to be a lovely day; I just needed to get into "date mode". I have never been good at this hand-holding, fluttering of the eyelashes stuff. But Scott didn't seem to care, so I stopped worrying about nothing.)

Deep breath. I emptied the glass as we pulled into the Amsterdam's Central Station. Exiting the train, we looked aghast at each other: there were masses of people in front of us, throngs of overflowing crowds. We could hardly move.

Making our way, we slowly exited the station and came out

to the street where there were even more people. Crowds and crowds of people. All wearing orange. What were all these people doing there? Was there a march? A protest? A parade?

I clapped my hands together. A parade? My fingers were crossed. (You can take the girl out of New Orleans but you cannot take the New Orleans out of the girl.) I looked at Scott, hopeful. He looked confused. He was not expecting this. And then he shrugged his shoulders, winked at me and went smiling to find out what was going on. He asked one of the many people wearing orange. With the answer, he turned to me with hands in the air, a victory sign.

It was not a parade. It was more than that.

It was jackpot.

It was Queen's Day.

THE day that the entire country of Holland parties. Young or old, no matter what age, or where, every single Dutch national was out on the streets to celebrate the birthday of their Queen.

The entire city of Amsterdam was flooded in orange, everyone dressed in their national color, all having a great time. There were coffee shops galore and even more bars, each with mobile beer taps, set up on the sidewalk. Djs were playing on every street corner.

And in between the bars and the djs, the locals had turned the remaining space outside their house into a flea market. To monitor the activities, they brought out their living room couch and a few garden chairs for their friends, and what would normally be a quiet flea market, turned into a house party. Streets and streets of house parties.

It was a massive block party covering the entire city. The entire country.

It was unbelievable. We had truly hit jackpot.

We followed the people down the streets, dancing with the music, our first beer in our hands. I bought us two orange feather boas. Under normal circumstances, I don't think Scott would have worn one, but the frivolity and celebratory atmosphere of Amsterdam was intoxicating.

Before long, the streets hit the canal. Again, we were floored.

"Look, Scott, look!" I pointed. You couldn't miss it. The party was on land and on water: a floating parade. One barge after another, decorated in orange, sailing through the canals. Each boat was full of people partying, each one with bigger speakers than the one before, all of them pumping music.

I was in heaven. There must have been a million people in the streets. Maybe more. Maybe two. In one giant massive celebration.

Needless to say, we did not visit any museums that day.

———

The party continued late into the night. All over the city. However, when the bars started to shut down, and the cleaning crews came in, we knew we needed to find a place to sleep.

We were tired, exhausted. We had been walking all over Amsterdam, dancing to every tune, drinking, and eating for more than 12 hours. Non-stop. I was ready for bed. I was crashing.

But first we needed to find a bed.

Which is not as easy as you'd think when you have no money. We were broke, having spent most of our money on beer and sausages. We pooled 35 dollars. Wherever we ended up was not going to be romantic, that was a given.

If we found a place, that is. We had walked into the Holland's biggest party of the year. A party worthy of people flying in from all over the country, from all over the world. It was only for three days. But it was worth it.

Needless to say, we were not the only travelers looking for a room, a place to stay.

Dismissing all the expensive hotels, we started calling round to the budget hotels. All the budget hotels were full. Hostels were booked. The city was in full occupancy. At least for any room that cost $35.

Actually we only had $25 left, since we decided to stop for some more beer and a hot dog.

It was way after midnight. Sitting on the side of the canal, we were wondering what should we do. Flipping the coin, heads won. We decided to wander the streets until we could get the first train back to Brussels. If we got tired of walking, we could go and sleep in the park. I was up for that.

Evidently, we got lost. We had no real destination and just walked to pass the hours, under street lights, over bridges, past the narrow houses and many canals. The city was silent now. It was so strange and yet so calming after the hedonism and excitement of the day.

Suddenly, after crossing one canal, the lights were no longer "white". No, there was a reddish glow coming from the windows and storefronts lining the street.

"Oh, how pretty! Look!" I said. My first thought was that it was a remnant of the day's orange extravaganza.

I looked closer. In every window there was a woman, sitting on a stool. Not wearing much.

Ahhhh.

The light was red. Not orange.

We were in the red-light district.

It took me a moment to process. Scott, not so much. He was horrified that we were there and tried to guide me away. I was not having it; I was curious. I had never been to a red-light district before and wanted to meet the prostitutes, these ladies of the night.

I had a few questions.

I wanted to find out what the price was for a blow job.

And, I also wanted to see if they had a room to spare.

––––––––––

We didn't stay the night, despite the hilarious conversations that ensued. Most of these ladies did not speak English, and trying to communicate in universal sign language through their "store fronts" led to much laughter. Between signing for blow jobs and ear plugs, they probably thought that I was asking after a threesome.

Uhm. No, thank you, ma'am. You see, I was on this date...

We left our new "best friends" and continued walking, holding hands, following the canals back into the city center.

The streets led to a park, but the gates were closed. Jumping the fence, we walked through the park, passing fountains and flower beds, before finding a little spot beneath the trees and a blanket of stars...

And "slept" there, until the morning came...

––––––––––

What an A++ day.

══════════

Lagniappe

When you are in Holland, you must drink the local "water": Heineken. Since we are there in spirit, it seems only right to enjoy one right now.

Along with the cold "pinche", I would suggest you have some bitterballen. It is hands down good. Like really good. Which is why when I am in Holland, I have it every day. No joke.

Even with 3 hours chill time, it is worth making. If I were you, I would get a six pack and invite your friends. It's party time.

I dare you to have any left over. Of the beer. Or the bitterballen.

Bitterballen

30 minutes with a 3 hour chill time

3 tablespoons butter
3 tablespoons flour
½ cup beef broth
1 beef top sirloin steak, cut into
    ½ inch cubes
¼ cup minced fresh parsley
¼ teaspoon salt
¼ ground nutmeg

⅛ teaspoon pepper
1⅓ cups dry bread crumbs
2 eggs
1 teaspoon milk
1 teaspoon canola oil
oil for frying
mustard for taste

1. In a large saucepan, melt butter over medium heat and stir in flour until smooth.

2. Add the broth, bringing it to a boil. Stir for 1 minute until thickened.

3. Slowly add meat and parsley.

4. Cook and stir until meat is no longer pink.

5. Add and stir in the salt, nutmeg, and pepper.

6. Put into a bowl and let sit in a fridge for 3 hours until chilled. (A pain, I know. Have a beer.)

———

7. Get two bowls. In one bowl, add the breadcrumbs. In another bowl, whisk together the eggs, milk, and oil.

8. Drop meat mixture into the breadcrumbs making a ball.

9. Take each ball and dip it into the egg mixture and then again into the crumbs.

———

10. Heat oil until sizzling (bread sizzles).

11. Fry balls, a few at a time, for 2 to 4 minutes until golden crispy brown on all sides.

12. Drain on kitchen paper and boom! You deserved the wait. Have one with a beer.

Dip it into mustard for an extra kick.

"Bones heal. Chicks dig scars. Pain is temporary. Glory is forever."

Evel Knieval

GOLF AIR

Somewhere in/over Former Yugoslavia

Cigar in my mouth, I took another look at my cards. Not my best hand. And I was in waaay deep. This might worry some poker players.

But not me. This game was one where I played the faces on the men, not just those on the cards.

Leaning back in my chair, I took the cigar out of my mouth and blew rings into the air. I loved it when I did that. When I was a teenager, my friends and I used to smoke outside my parents' garage. It took me months to master blowing smoke rings. But when I did, I never smoked any other way.

It was about that time when I learned how to play poker.

The reading of faces took a while longer. But when you make a few mistakes, you pay more attention to certain details: body language, changes in breath, involuntary twitches, squinting of the eyes with displeasure. The body tells you all you need to know; it never lies.

Tonight, I was hoping that "I am lying" in silent body talk is universally the same the world over. No matter the spoken language.

Because I do not speak Serbian. Or Russian. I do not speak Greek. And Arabic is way beyond me.

What I do speak is cards. Just cards.

Where was I?

Close to the UN Army barracks in Yugoslavia. Some of us were part of the UN Peacekeeping Corps in Bosnia. Some of us were not. Some of us sold guns. Some of us did not. Some us reported the truth. Some of us did not. Needless to say, there were no virgins amongst us.

What we did for a living made no difference tonight. Our lives were about the cards this evening. And tonight, I needed to win.

Tonight, I wanted to win.

We did not gamble for money. None of us had the kind of money that would make this game interesting, heighten the blood pressure, make the hands sweat.

Gambling for paper is a soft thrill. It is not who we were. It was not how we rolled.

The stakes were different. At the beginning of the game, we each wrote on a piece of paper what we wanted. Our wishes were then placed into an envelope, which was put aside for safekeeping.

The one with the most chips at the end of the night would win his wish. Whatever he wanted, whatever he had written down on the piece of paper, he would get. And we would have to get it for him. We would make it happen.

That was the pledge. No matter how crazy.

And mine was crazy alright.

But it was a good crazy. No drugs, no women.

I wanted to play golf. I had a hankering for it. And there was this beautiful course on the other side of the mountain range.

In enemy territory.

My boys would have to parachute me and my golf clubs. Each of us separately. And not just me. For I was not playing alone. We were all going. The loser would have to arrange a drop of four men and four sets of golf clubs.

Where would we get the golf clubs? Silly question. That was not a problem. The least of my worries. Of course, I had my clubs with me. I came prepared for war.

Moreover, it was not just about the drop off. Of four people and four golf bags. After the game, they would have to arrange for air transport to come and pick us up.

In enemy territory.

A few moments later, I hid my smile as I blew a smoke ring and watched it hover our heads before it disappeared.

They did not know it yet, but I was winning.

I did not need to know what cards they had or read their faces.

I had a Full House.

I cannot confirm or deny what happened that day.

But I will say this.

I love it when a plan comes together.

Lagniappe

Now to my knowledge, food is not served at poker games. I could be wrong but most of the time, it is a diet of tobacco and alcohol: cigars, cigarettes, beer, whiskey, really whatever is your poison. Choosing a recipe for this story was challenging. Especially since the 19th hole is exactly of the same dietary persuasion as that of the poker game.

In other words, just pour yourself a drink.

And practice blowing smoke rings.

You might even want to learn how to play poker or golf.

The jumping out of planes is completely optional.

"Maybe that's what life is...a wink of the eye and winking stars."

Jack Kerouac

DIAMONDS AND FUR IN THE SAHARA
Algeria

"Oh, God. It's hot," I said.

"Obviously, nothing to do with the fur coat you are wearing," remarked one friend on the camel next to me. "In the middle of the Sahara," he continued.

Smart ass.

I sighed. Nothing investigative about this journalist. Men. They didn't appreciate that fur keeps the body cool as much as it warms. However, looking back, I must concede that it probably was a bit over the top. At the time, I thought is was perfectly appropriate.

Besides, I prefer to dress the part.

After pulling up my hijab in order to cover my face against the sand, I flicked my wrists in order to urge my camel forward through the thick sands.

Of the Sahara.

We were somewhere south of Tamanrasset, more than that I did not know. We were halfway between somewhere and nowhere. I did know that we were literally in the middle of the desert.

Of the Sahara.

I was not complaining. It was beautiful. The flatness of the earth, covered with a blanket of countless rocks crushed by time, as far as the eye could see. And then beyond: the sand continued over the edge, in waves of rolling flatness. Such an acronym, but there is no other way to describe the sensation of where we were.

There were a few times, and really only a few, when we would pass a great big rock, rising like a giant out of the land of crystals. I wondered if the rock was the last remnant of what was once a huge land structure that, despite having held its own against centuries of sun, had lost against the winds of change. And thus was transformed piece by piece, one kernel at a time, into the blanket of sand that we were crossing.

I was grateful for these rock formations. It meant that we were not lost and on the right track. Like the sailors of old who charted their course using the stars, the Touaregs charted their course using the few remaining rock formations scattered throughout their home, the Sahara desert.

Personally, I really hoped that our Touareg guide, Ahmed, was not just navigating by the stars and the rocks. However, I was not 100% sure whether he owned a GPS. Or if he owned any other "don't get lost" tool like a compass or a map. As much as my gypsy heart would love the scenario of navigating by the stars, the thought of getting permanently lost curdled fear in the lower part of my back.

Silently, I assured myself that we are in the 21st century and Touaregs must be active participants in technology. One could also say that this is what blind trust looks like.

Every once in awhile, Ahmed would threaten my sanity and say he could not find his compass. Touareg humor. "Very funny, ha ha," I replied.

I had a compass. It might be as big as my thumbnail and hung on my key chain but it worked. However, after a few hours in the sand, I knew that I was completely and utterly out of my depth.

Ergo, wherever Ahmed went, so did I. Actually the camel followed him and I was sitting on it.

In my fur coat.

———

Now before we start the story, it is probably best to give some context.

Many moons ago, I worked as a journalist in Algeria. I was sent to cover a series of stories about Algeria during a time of revolution, rebellion, and sporadic moments of peace. After a few months of my residency, work and curiosity had taken me to the towns, villages, and cities that decorated the Mediterranean coast. But, I had never been south.

South into the desert.

I had heard the siren call of the Sahara. I wanted to understand these people, this nation. And since you will never understand a fisherman if you have not been on the water, the same goes for the people of the Maghreb, the many nations of people that are defined by interaction skirting the desert of Sahara, this massive sea of sand that covers the width of the entire continent of Africa.

There is no shortage of literature, poems, stories, myths that herald the Sahara. I had read many and heard even more.

The siren song of the Sahara was strong. I heard it loud and clear.

———

We were four journalists who coordinated our schedules in order to take two weeks off and get lost. Our intention was clear: heed the song and follow the siren into the waves of sand. We wanted to listen to the stories of the Touaregs, the indigenous people of the Sahara. We wanted to drink the mint tea, boiled from handmade fires and poured with great flair several feet above the tiny glass. We wanted to sleep under the carpet of stars on a blanket of gentle rocks.

Conception is one thing; preparation was a little bit more difficult. Preparation is always difficult for the unprepared.

I happened to be an addict to the adrenaline of last minute scramble. In those days, being unprepared could be explained away as being "busy" or "flexible". My time was consumed with interviewing the President and the leader of the rebels in between dodging friendly fire. I assure you: finding a sleeping bag was not #1 on my to do list.

Still, I thought it would be easy. What I should have thought was, is it easy to find a sleeping bag at 4 p.m., the night before our departure? In a country which did not have sporting goods stores? The key word is "sand" in this part of the world. Not "mountains".

My compatriots, however, loved this stuff and were ridiculously prepared. They brought their 20 gallon backpack and Antarctic sleeping bag with them everywhere. On every trip. On every mission. It was borderline obnoxious.

Me? I was all about glamour. The glamour and the risk and the adventure of being a journalist in Africa was tremendous, never overwhelming, and always welcome. It was my catnip. The kind of journalist that looked like he never slept, never washed, and always drank and drugged - that was not me. (And there were/are many who subscribe to that particular attire, religiously, like a monk would wear his robes. I think they do it in order to be easily recognizable and therefore revered.)

In fact, I was the anomaly. The majority were alcoholic adrenaline junkies. Wait a second. Who am I fooling? We all were alcoholic adrenaline junkies.

The difference was I just wanted to do it in high heels, fur, and diamonds.

As far as I was concerned, someone else could wear khaki.

———

I do not need my mother to tell me that doing everything last minute, and not preparing in advance will leave you with an empty plate, with a side of empty-handed. However, if there is medal for great expectations and awards for great efforts, sign me up and make the statue in my honor.

I will say that I did try. Very hard. The minute the last interview of the day finished, I shucked all responsibility of the job and raced down the steps of the government building. I jumped into my car which had all my staples for a successful search: full tank of gas, a full bottle of whiskey, bottles of coke, packs of cigarettes, and a working radio playing Rai music. (Who says I am not prepared?)

I had 5 hours before everything closed, and in that time, I covered all of Algiers. I do not believe in mission impossible.

No mission is ever impossible.

Remember, these are the days before Google when the only way you are going to find anything is by using your legs, going from one store to another. The mission called for some good old fashioned detective work: asking one person after another for a sleeping bag. We went up and down central Algiers in every small shop on the corner, around the corner from the minaret, underneath canopies of hanging copperware while occasionally stopping for a quick glass of tea and coffee.

It was a race against time. The best kind.

You can imagine the conversations that were had when looking for a sleeping bag, and your French and Arabic is misunderstood. Sleeping bag versus "sleeping" in a "bag".

Clearly, different. Not everyone agreed.

And when Algiers closed down for the night, we did not give up. I took the search to the hotel where I was staying. I asked friends, hotel employees random guests, and barflys.

I can confirm with confidence that arms dealers do not have sleeping bags.

I think they should and told them so.

Diamonds and Fur in the Sahara

Algeria

"Oh, God. It's hot," I said.

"Obviously, nothing to do with the fur coat you are wearing," remarked one friend on the camel next to me. "In the middle of the Sahara," he continued.

Smart ass.

I sighed. Nothing investigative about this journalist. Men. They didn't appreciate that fur keeps the body cool as much as it warms. However, looking back, I must concede that it probably was a bit over the top. At the time, I thought is was perfectly appropriate.

Besides, I prefer to dress the part.

After pulling up my hijab in order to cover my face against the sand, I flicked my wrists in order to urge my camel forward through the thick sands.

Of the Sahara.

We were somewhere south of Tamanrasset, more than that I did not know. We were halfway between somewhere and no-where. I did know that we were literally in the middle of the desert.

Of the Sahara.

I was not complaining. It was beautiful. The flatness of the earth, covered with a blanket of countless rocks crushed by

The next morning, my organized friends decided to meet early for breakfast. Bright and sparky. (Who is bright and sparky in the morning?... Exactly...) Their bags were packed and thermoses full. They were dressed as if they were about fly up Mount Everest. 'Fly' being the operative word here. The three of them were Dr. Gadget clones. They obviously took adventure differently. They took it seriously.

I had woke up in a different state of mind.
I was not alone, which is not bad.
I had a hangover, which was not great.
I still had no sleeping bag.
I had to get dressed, find sleeping arrangements, and then get downstairs before the car to the airport took off.
Focus, focus. Focus.
One thing at a time.

I might not have found a sleeping bag, but I did have something to wear. Oh yeah, baby. I had found and obtained several Touareg dresses, including the long scarves appropriate for the Sahara sand and sun.

Dressed and desperate, the situation called for creativity. If I could not find a sleeping bag, I was going to bring the hotel bed with me.

Easy. Problem solved.

Slamming back a coffee, with a cigarette in my mouth and my sunglasses on, I closed the door and was ready for this amazing encounter with my siren - el Sahara. She was singing to me.

I literally could not wait.

After getting to the airport, we started the process of getting our tickets and going through security. Given the circumstances of the rebellion, the army was manually checking every bag. No guns. Check. We were journalists. We had pens, not swords.

Before long, we boarded a small twin engine plane and flew south. The plane had a particular chugging sound, kind of like the "Little Engine that Could". I think I can, I think I can, not die. In other words, we did not really "fly", we "chugged" south. One of the engines might not have been as effective as the other.

But no worries, we got there. I had donned my head scarf on the plane, ready to enter the jurisdiction of the Sahara winds. Sunglasses on, hair and face protected by the scarf, tagelmust, I descended from the plane to take my first real look at the Sahara.

At first, I could not see anything. Or hardly anything. It was as if I had entered a tunnel, into a warp-like existence. It was as if I was being transported while standing still. Everything was moving. The air had taken on form, sand and light were whisping around me. There was only one colour, no matter where you looked. The color of sand. Constant and comprehensive.

Sand was everywhere, except when you looked up. And then you were hit by the piercing blue sky. It was not the sun which I expected to hurt my eyes, but the intensity of the sky which was blinding.

That crystal depth of blue. A profound lightness of being.

Oh, how I do love the sky.

The heat was dense with texture. I could feel the heat penetrate my bones and caress my lungs. The heat permeated everything, as if to say to the body, "You are mine now". This ownership was welcome, especially to me - someone who is physically always cold because of extremely low blood pressure. I could feel how the heat took over and my body relaxed, in comfort at last.

It was an awesome moment: coming off the airplane, sucking in the heat, breathing the sand, center to the dry whirlwind, peering out over the horizon of barren nothing, and then looking up at the blinding blue of the sky.

Sigh.

I crouched down, grabbing the sand in my hands, rubbing it together, absorbing the sensation while amazed at how soft it was.

I was exactly where I should be.

———————

We drove for hours east into the desert. Further and further into the Sahara, not stopping until we had come to an oasis. It was the village of our guide, Ahmed's home.

It was here we were to start our journey on camelback through the Sahara.

Camels are beautiful animals in their eccentricity. I love them because they are different and perfect for their environment. Have you ever noticed that the color of camels is the same color as the sand?

Having spent significant time in Sub-Saharan Africa, I thought to myself, in comparison, there are no large animals that are green. They are black and white, pink, grey, even polka dot. But none of the animals are the same color as their environment.

But in the Sahara, camels are. They are the same color as the sand they walk on. With long legs, they carry gallons of water along with precious cargo of food and people on their back. I found camels to be incredibly noble.

They might have bad breath but they are noble all the same. I went to introduce myself, as one would to a horse. My camel for the journey had a long Arabic name. So, I asked for his forgiveness and called him Sam, for short.

Less than a half an hour after our arrival at the oasis, we mounted our camels, packed with our luggage and started walking further east. I had my tagelmust scarf on, because although the wind had died down, it was not enough to warrant not covering your face. Despite the welcome heat, inhaling small rocks on a continual basis does not sit well with my lungs. (Said the smoker.)

Nothing prepared me for the sunset though. Holy Crayola Box.

It was color everywhere.
360 sunset.
Surround sound sunset.
It was as if God had taken gallons and gallons of paint of every color and threw it against the wall of the sky.
It was glorious.

We stopped for several minutes in silence, in wonder.

Ahmed, our Touareg guide, smiled in pride.

"Welcome to my backyard," he said, before turning to spur his camel forward.

About an hour later, we stopped and made camp. Ahmed started a fire and boiled water for tea. The rest of us were given jobs to do, including setting up our sleeping bags. Given that the temperature was already dropping, it seemed that the best place to lay my "sleeping bag" would be near the fire.

My friends unwrapped their sleeping bags, which looked like multi-colored plastic worm holes. As you know, mine was a little different. Unzipping my bag, I took out my bed. I literally unrolled my bed. That morning I had taken the bed sheets, blankets and pillows from my hotel room, rolled them up and stuffed them in a bag.

Beggars can be choosers.

Ahmed came over, giving me a cup of freshly made mint tea, laughing that he had never seen a bed like mine before. "Why not?" I asked. It made perfect sense. To me at least.

I am not sure if Ahmed was referring to the bed or the fur. The final touch was my fur coat on top, which would act as my extra blanket against the cold.

Comfortable and warm, I snuggled underneath my hotel blankets and fur. Sighing with happiness, I looked up at the sky, heavy with millions of stars. I had never felt so close to the universe before.

The difference between a midnight star gaze with 20 stars in the sky and 20 million stars in the sky, is the Sahara.

Lucky me.

––––––––––

Early to bed, early to rise. There are no shades in the Sahara. No blackout curtains. When the sun is up, it is up. And kind of hard to ignore.

A giant blazing ball of heat.

After a breakfast of dates and coffee, the plan was to pull together our make shift camp and be on our way. We wanted to get as far as we could before midday when the sun was its hottest.

I rolled up my bed and pushed it back into the bag. Struggling with the zipper, I jumped up and down on it to make sure it would fit.

My friends were smiling at me, amused. I cheekily told them that they were jealous. And they were. I could hear their teeth chatter last night. (Ok, I am exaggerating a bit. They didn't chatter. It just makes the story better for me.)

Bed rolled and fur stuffed, I tried to climb on top of Sam. Several times. 'Elegant' and 'Graceful' are not words I would use to describe my attempts. 'Incompetent' in mounting a camel would be more descriptive.

Try, try again if at first you don't succeed. Before long, Sam and I followed Ahmed out.

And single file, we walked into the desert.

––––––––––

When you are ride for hours in the blazing heat, through seas of sand, you have time to philosophize. Being immersed in barren land is something quite disturbing for the soul. Maybe not disturbing but rather challenging.

You are used to seeing life all around you, whether it be urban life or the civilized life of nature. You are used to lush forests, mountains that touch the sky, fields that extend as far as the eye can see and oceans with no horizon, where the waves chase each other endlessly.

With the novelty of the Sahara, I was realizing that I had taken life for granted, wherever I saw it. I expected to see life. It had never registered with me that I live on a planet made of living things. Being surrounded by the lack of life was like being slapped awake.

The Sahara used to be a sea bed. All that life left when the ocean disappeared, leaving this barren land.

This beautiful barren land.

And so, I started looking for life everywhere, wanting to celebrate it.

I am pleased, so pleased to say that I found it. (Funny how that works: when you start looking, you find.)

I started to see life in the most difficult place to live. My natural curiosity went into overdrive. When I saw birds that flew overhead, I thought to myself: where do they nest? I saw the crabs that lived in the sand, I thought: what do they eat? I was seeing life everywhere. And I wanted to know more. How was it possible? It was more than just finding life. It was metaphysical. If life could exist in this barren land, then life did not die. Hope would never die. Life persisted despite all conditions.

I wanted to find everything and anything to prove my philosophical theory. In the largest desert in the world, I wanted to prove that life has no death, that hope survives the absence of everything. Nature had given me the greatest invitation.

I had so many questions. I could have inhaled entire Encyclopedias and years of National Geographics.

But I had something even better: Ahmed.

He knew everything. Literally everything. Ahmed was more

than a walking talking compass. He was a walking-talking-treasure chest of knowledge. Ahmed loved to talk and show us around 'his backyard'. It was truly an amazing learning experience for the inquisitive mind.

———

A few days into our safari, we saw a dome on the horizon. Ahmed stated it was the makeshift home of a Touareg. I was thinking, how do they live here? On what? What do they eat?

Naturally, we slowed and stopped. Ahmed gave the women water and some of our food. Apparently, the men were out hunting and the women were staying at home, their dome. (What were they hunting? I do not know.)

A verbal exchange took place. Being the curious cat that I am, I enquired what they were talking about. One of the women was in pain. From what I deduced, she was suffering from menstrual cramps. I knew exactly how she felt.

I clapped my hands to draw attention to myself. "Ahmed! I have something. Sam! Let me down!"

The camel kneeled and I slid off, looking for my bag. I was searching for a something that could help her. Which was of course on the bottom of the bag. I had to take out the bed, the sheets and my personal effects. I emptied them all out onto the sand, at last finding the little box I was looking for.

Which held my headache pills. My magic pain reliever pills. They were over the counter but packed a punch in delivering me from pain every month. Or from every hangover I have ever had, much like the morning of our departure.

I opened the box and offered them to the lady in pain.

With Ahmed's help in translation, she accepted them with a smile. I told her that it would take twenty minutes but she would feel fine and not to worry, that she could trust the ibuprofen. There was concern on her face as I spoke, telling Ahmed to tell her not to worry.

I then realized that perhaps she had never had pain relievers before. That this monthly extreme pain was her normal. That would not be a stretch of reality: we were in the middle of the Sahara and she did live in a dome.

I asked Ahmed and she nodded. My heart broke for her and for the countless women who live like this, especially when we take popping a pill for granted. I wanted to do more but it would have to wait until we got back. Sighing, I turned to start packing the bag with my strewn belongings.

My friend's laughter broke through my thoughts.

"Christina?"

"Yes?" I huffed, while stuffing my bed back into the bag.

"What was in that box?" He asked, high on his camel.

"Headache pills," I answered. Duh. Didn't he just see what happened?

"And what else? What did I see shining?" He was smiling as if he knew the answer.

Sigh. I knew what I was in for.

"Uhm, diamonds." If I had to answer him, I was going to work it.

"What? You bought diamonds to the desert?" The others, of course, had to chirp in.

"Yes," I replied. I had to defend myself. "My room was burgled last week and I did not want to leave them in the safe. So, I packed them in my little headache pill box for safekeeping. It is all perfectly normal."

"Right," they replied. "Perfectly normal. It is perfectly normal for you to bring diamonds and fur to the desert along with your five star bed. Perfectly normal."

Perfectly normal. Indeed.

Just like me.

―――――――

Lagniappe

Couscous is a staple dish throughout Algeria and the Maghreb region. Easy to make and simple to prepare. There are many variations of this dish, but for this particular recipe, I chose the basic one: vegetables. You can add lamb, chicken, or fish. As you like.

Making the couscous itself is super easy. Add boiling water to couscous in a bowl and cover it for 10 minutes. 1.5 to 1 : water to couscous ratio. Fluff and serve. It is like instant coffee but not.

The sauce that goes together with the couscous is what takes time. 2 to 3 hours at times. So, this is one that you would start making after lunch and let it soak and simmer throughout the afternoon in time for dinner. It is worth the wait.

Enjoy a few glasses of mint tea in the meantime. Try pouring it into your glass from high, like Ahmed did in the Sahara.

Algerian Vegetable Couscous

2.5 hours

1 large onion, chopped
½ teaspoon turmeric
¼ teaspoon cayenne
½ cup vegetable stock
½ tablespoon cinnamon
1½ teaspoon pepper
½ teaspoon salt
5 tablespoons tomato purée
4 garlic cloves
3 medium zucchini
4 small squash
1 carrot
4 medium potatoes
1 red bell pepper
1 can garbanzo beans

1. In a large pot, saute the onion in the vegetable stock.
2. Add all the spice and tomato paste and simmer for 2 minutes.
3. Add all the vegetables (chopped), stir for 1 minute before covering the entire mixture with water.
4. Let simmer for 2 hours.
5. Ten minutes before the end, stir in the beans.
6. Done. Add the stew on top of the couscous. Do not mix in.

Note: For extra flavor, use the water from the stew to make the couscous.

I usually have this with chilled red wine, especially if it is hot outside.

"There is no substitute for hard work."

Thomas Edison

DIRT UNDERNEATH MY FINGERNAILS
Alaska, USA

"You've got to be kidding me! You want us to do what?" I was shocked.

Wait, a second! Whoa, whoa, whoa. My brain was putting the brakes on what I had just heard because it was not what I thought I had come to do.

Here being Alaska.

"I'd like you to take the stones out of the dirt. I have several tons of dirt coming from a nearby friend down the road. Instead of buying dirt, I want you to take the stones out of Roger's dirt before mixing it with fertilizer. Once you are finished, we will use it to landscape the front yard." Bob was very pleased with himself. He thought it was a great idea, saving money.

Me? Not so much.

Let me repeat. He wanted us to take stones out of dirt. Aren't stones supposed to be in dirt? I was not computing. I had just woken up, exhausted after the two day journey from Brussels where I had left with an image in my head of a glorious adventure in the wilds of Alaska. I was going to get away from the snobby aristo-eurocrats of Brussels and be with real people, real life in the last outpost of purism of those who seek hard adventure: Alaska. Capital A for Adventure and Alaska.

It was going to be a wonderful four months, working while enjoying the fantastic sports and experiences that God's backyard can offer: fishing, hiking, kayaking, camping. It was going to be amazing, or so I thought.

Manual labour was not really part of my plan. I mean, it was not in the postcard of working vacation I thought I was on. Waitressing is one thing, but sifting through dirt is another.

Nancy interrupted my mental meandering as she leaned over, with a pan in her hands, "Eggs, dear?"

"Yes, ma'am. Please." I was hungry, tired, and now very confused. We were sitting around the breakfast table, drinking coffee in the early morning. I thought I signed up for working on vacation, not working on the railroad.

Nope. Obviously other plans were made. I swallowed my bite of eggs.

No glory-filled adventure here. It sounded more like hard work. Lots of it. I was going to be taking stones out of dirt. Literally stones out of dirt.

Welcome to Alaska.

———

After a couple of cups of coffee, we all piled into the truck to pick up the dirt. By now, I was reconciled with the idea of the stones and the work involved. The stones would be large, which meant that the first step would be to move them away to the side. The rest would be easy. All we had to do was shovel the dirt into sacks for transportation. Estimating the work, I thought this cannot be so bad. A few big rocks and there are a few of us to do the work. This should go fast.

Right?

I should have added something strong to my coffee. A shot of anything. Alcoholic.

Arriving at Bob's neighbor's house, we parked in his driveway. Bob exited and we scooted along the front seat in order to follow in his wake. He went up to Roger (the neighbor), vigorously shaking his hand while clapping him on the back.

Boom! Boom! The sound of their greeting was loud, like lighting bolts. I was used to the soft demeanor of Europeans and their kisses on the cheek. Men in Alaska come in all different sizes, but only one size when it comes to spirit: huge. And it emanated from them, each and every one. I was surrounded by giants.

Roger began to show us around. It was a beautiful house, overlooking the strait in Ketchikan. So gorgeous. The light playing off the tips of the water waves, the sun playing hide-and-seek amongst the clouds, leaving the rainbow to connect mountain tops. This is how the earth must have been at the beginning. God's paradise.

After the tour, Roger took us to the all to the back. He pointed to a huge pile - scratch that - a mountain of dirt on the side of the house.

"Uhm, ok," I thought to myself, "He has landscaping to do. Where are these big rocks he wants us to take care of?"

Bob called us over to the pile.

"This is it! Let's go to work!" he said, while asking me to get the shovels in the back of the truck. I hauled them in my arms back to where he was standing.

Looking down, I asked "Where are the rocks?"

Bob looked at me, puzzled. "In the dirt, Christina."

I looked down again.

Those were not rocks. Those were pebbles.

Thousands of them.

A shovel was not going to help at all. I would have to get on my hands and knees in the dirt and take out each pebble, one at a time.

Oh. Joy.

I had to have a plan of how to do accomplish this. Rake first and then sieve.
It would be liking digging for gold.

Except there was no gold.

This tiny chore would take an entire week, from beginning to end. It was backbreaking work. The kind I was not used to. Which made it so important.

Spending large amounts of time on your knees hurts. The back aches to a point where you have to make the decision that you can either lie down and rest, or you decide to rally in order to get the job done by grinning and bearing it. The hands hurt from cramping. My body was in pain.

But I would not complain. Very quickly, it occurred to me that this job was not an accident. Bob could afford dirt. I knew it was a lesson, a test to check my work ethic from the pansy hands one gets from lack of manual labor.

Don't worry. I got the message loud and clear.

Lesson number one was a warning: this could be me for the rest of my life if I did not get an education.

Lesson number two was to be humble and respect those who do manual labour in order to put food on the table.

Lesson number three was nothing beats hard work. Hard work is what makes the world go round. There is great integrity and pride in a job well done, especially if it is done with your hands.

Work was not foreign to me. I had always worked. I mean, I was putting myself through school. I didn't get any handouts; I grew up on government subsidies.

During my time in Alaska, I would be completely and utterly busy with work. And I loved every second of it. Early morning hours would be archiving for an insurance company and then off to continue working at the fishery where I would gut and clean the salmon, getting it ready for freezing. (Lots of laughs on that assembly line.) If I was not at the fishery, I would be working at the local diner, serving my regulars: lumberjacks, the fishermen, the hunters. I loved it, yamming it up with a wink and smile, asking them in my sweetest Southern accent if they wanted "leaded or unleaded" coffee.

Every day was full on. I think I might have had three days off in total of the four months. Saving every penny for my tuition, I was a workaholic. The good kind. I was addicted to a job well done.

And strangely, it probably was the chore of clearing dirt which kicked it all into overdrive.

And the people. I was surrounded by amazing people. Humbled by them. By their approach to work, by their integrity, by their grit and tenacity. I was definitely on another planet, far from eurocrats of Brussels. Here in Alaska, there was one currency: hard work. The real kind.

Like attracts like. All the people that I met had migrated like a magnet to the Upper 48. A place of opportunity where hard work is recognized, beer is cold, and coffee is strong. No matter the background or what happened to them in their past, it was their work, their sweat and strength which was welcome here. The stories of the people manning the fishing boats or the lumber yards were those of trials and tribulations, each one looking for a second chance. Or a third. Or sometimes a 10th. It did not matter. If you were willing to work with your hands, you would be given a chance to earn a living. Hard work with dedication is the great leveler and ever the great riser.

The sense of pride from working manual labor was real and tangible; it emanated from every single person that I met in Alaska. Saint and sinner alike. At the end of the day, I am sure they kept company with their demons instead of chasing angels. But come sunrise, they showed up at the sawmill, the airport, the port, the fisheries. And worked. And got their hands dirty.

That their brows were heavy with worry, or that their feet were in pain from serving double shifts, did not mean that there was an absence of laughter, or affection. There also was a generosity of heart and wallet. It seemed those who had it the hardest were the always the first to stand up and help.

Over the coming months, my esteem and respect only grew for the working man and woman. They became my heros. They still are. For me they are the realest thing, humanity at its purest. We should all aim to be like them.

I know these people are not just in Alaska, but everywhere: throughout the United States, Russia, China, Asia, Africa or throughout Europe and in South America. Anywhere in the world. They are the pillars of our civilization, working hard to make a living for themselves, for their family, for a visible chance at a better life.

Do you know how you can find them?

You can recognize them by the dirt under their fingernails.

PS. Do me a favor will you? When you do meet them, buy them a beer for me.

Lagniappe

While reading this chapter, I would have a cup of black coffee. Or a beer after work. Definitely something strong. (I never saw anyone drink Cherry Cola in Alaska.) Lift a glass to yourself for all the hard work you do.

And I hope you are hungry because I could not make up my mind which recipe to share with you, so you get both. Oh yeah, baby…

Drunk Fish
15 minutes

½ lb. Halibut cheeks
2 tablespoons butter
2 tablespoons dry vermouth
½ lemon
Season: salt, pepper and fresh dill

1. Melt the butter together with the vermouth and ½ lemon in a saute pan.

2. Saute the halibut for one minute on one side while you season with salt and pepper.

3. Turn over and lower heat while you cook the fish for 8 minutes per inch. Have a glass of white wine while you wait.

When the fish turns flaky it is done. Overcooked halibut tastes like old shoe. Don't go there.

And... drumroll... the classic...the best...my favorite: grilled cheese and tomato soup.

Grilled Cheese
15 minutes

Bread
Butter
Cheese

(I did not put amounts because it is all up to you.)

1. Butter the inside and the outside of the bread. Add as much cheese as you want.

2. Melt loads of butter in a pan over medium heat. Grill one side of the sandwich.

3. Add more butter to the pan. Flip the sandwich over until cheese starts is melted and start oozing out. Unbelievably good.

Note: to shake things up a bit - try different cheeses, add chilis or jalapenos, ham or bacon, tomatoes, as you like. But the classic is classic for a reason.

Tomato Soup

50 minutes

Now for those who are against Campbell's tomato soup, here is one you can make at home.

½ cup extra virgin olive oil
1 onion
1 fennel bulb
4 spring thyme (or thyme seasoning)
3 tablespoons tomato paste
4 cups water
2 cans peeled Italian tomatoes
Season with salt and pepper

1. In a large pot, heat the olive oil and saute the chopped onion, fennel and thyme

2. When they are softened, add the tomato paste. Cook and stir.

3. Add the water and tomatoes; bring to a boil.

4. Reduce the heat to a simmer for 30 minutes, while stirring occasionally.

5. When it is reduced by ⅓, it is ready.

Now, you can either blend it all for a smooth tomato soup or blend half and keep it a bit chunky. As you wish.

"You're mad. Bonkers.
Off your head...But I
will tell you a secret...
All the best people are."

Lewis Carroll's
Alice in Wonderland

THE BRASS AND THE BOMB

Solomon Islands

"Honey?!" My husband called to me from inside the house. He had just come home and was pouring himself a drink.

It was warm night, as most nights were in the Solomon Islands. I was relaxing outside on the porch with an ice tea, waiting for him to join me.

"Yes, love?" He sounded a bit distressed, which was worrying. Simon was usually the most chilled out person ever.

I walked into the house and saw him paralyzed, staring at me.

Now I was really worried. "What is wrong, honey?"

He pointed to the fireplace.

I turned, confused. Why was he pointing to the fireplace?

Oh, good. He noticed the surprise. I was quite happy with my work; the flowers added a nice touch.

"Honey? What are 6 bombs doing on our fireplace?" he asked.

"Oh, those old things? I found them this morning. When I was gardening. I dug them up," I replied nonchalantly.

What was the big deal? They were old brass shells which I found while gardening this morning. I told him yesterday that I was going to plant. We needed a garden. Food was a scarcity on the island, coming occasionally by ship. Sometimes, the most expensive thing on the island could be a cup of sugar. Sadly, I could not grow sugar. But I could grow tomatoes. Or guava.

But enough about my garden. Simon did not seem to care about the garden. He was pointing to the 6 bombshells that lined the fireplace, resplendent with flowers.

"I dug them up, cleaned them off, and polished them. I made them into flower vases. Aren't they pretty?"

I was very proud of myself. Those shells were encrusted with dirt and took some scrubbing.

The whiskey in his drink now splashed all over the floor.

"You what? You crazy woman! Those are World War II bombs. They did not go off during the war, but it does not mean they never will." He was shaking his head in stupefaction.

"Ah," I said. From nonchalant to petrified in less than a millisecond.

"Ok. So, what do we do?" turning to him for guidance.

My husband was having convulsions, sweating bullets. He probably thought I was as dumb as a doornail and in this instance, he was definitely right.

The Solomon Islands was the battle ground for much of the fiercest fighting between the Axis and the Allied troops in the Pacific during World War II. Little did I know that this peaceful island, steeped in tradition and culture, was also the burial ground to thousands and thousands of mines and even more unexploded bombs.

I did not know this. I was young. Naive.

I blame youth.

My husband blames my brains.

However, whenever I tell this story, I don't talk about how ridiculous or how stupid I felt afterwards, or the fear of the bomb exploding while we transported each one, a single centimeter at a time outside of the house, lifting them so very gingerly off the fireplace, across the living room, onto the porch, down the stairs of the house and really really slowly over the gravel into the woods out back, finally laying the bomb down gently on the grass. Before returning to the house to do it another 5 times. I think it would be fair to say that we each had several heart attacks that night.

I do not share those particular details when I tell this story.

What I do say was that I was the badass that dug up a bomb, polished the brass, and put 6 of them on our fireplace. How many people can say that? Huh? Not many people.

Right. That is what I thought.

I never tell them that what happened next was probably the scariest 30 minutes of my life. You do not need to know that. All you need to know is that the brass was shiny when I was done with it.

And I lived to tell the tale.

———————

Lagniappe

I don't think they had a glass of milk after they cleared their house of bombs. So, join them with a glass of whiskey.

And when you are hungry, try this recipe out. The local delicacies of the Solomon Islands are some of my favorite foods. I love fresh papaya with yogurt and honey in the morning, and who can say no to baked banana with chocolate inside? But for this recipe I chose a dish which has it all: chicken, papaya, and coconut. Yum.

Papaya and Coconut Chicken
15 minutes

8 boneless, skinless chicken breast halves, cut into cubes
1 papaya, peeled and sliced
1¾ cup coconut milk (fresh or canned)
1 onion, chopped

1. In heated olive oil in a pan, cook the chicken until almost done which is approximately 5 minutes.

2. Add the onion, stirring the mixture until the onion becomes transparent.

3. Add the papaya and cook for another 5 minutes.

4. Remove the pan from heat before adding the coconut milk.

Serve with sweet potato (mashed or baked) or fried plantains (cousin of the banana - fried in oil over high heat).

I literally can taste this now.

"I believe that every human has a finite number of heartbeats. I don't intend to waste any of mine running around doing exercises."

Neil Armstrong

NOTHING TO PROVE
Nepal

Thank. You.
Thank.
You.
Thank.
You.
Thank.
You.
With every step, I kept pace with my prayer: Thank you.

I was going to get up this mountain. Nothing was going to stop me. Not the boulders. Not the ice. Not the cold. And not the altitude sickness.

I was going to get up this damn mountain.

Some call it Everest.

I call it the "damn mountain".

———

If you had asked me two months before trekking up that "damn mountain" if I thought I was going to be climbing Everest, I would have laughed. I would have literally put down anything I was holding in order to grab my stomach and fold over in giggles. Hysterics.

"You are so funny!" I would definitely exclaim. "I hate hiking!"

Truer words have never been spoken. If I get to choose between staying in bed and having sex, or hiking up a mountain in the cold to take in the fresh air. I am sorry, people. I choose sex. Call me partial.

Hiking has the ability to test my limits and bring out the worst in me. You can't talk because you are panting out of breath. There is no water. No sofas. And no taxi to take you back. YouknowwhatIamsayin'?

Run. Yes. Hike. No. I actually prefer any other sport.

Which is why it is curious that I not only hike but choose large mountain masses to climb. It is as if I have something to prove: I must conquer what I hate. Weird, I know. (There are therapists for this. Which is why I prefer to stay in bed and have sex. Cheaper.)

But sometimes life has lessons it wants you to learn, and puts people in your life to make them happen. Damn them and bless them at the same time.

———————

Roger is an retired Colonel of the British Army and upon reaching a certain age, he sold everything he had in England and moved to Hong Kong. Which is where we met. One evening, we ended up sitting next to each other at a speech hosted by the Royal Geographic Society, themed: "How adventurous are you?" (It was a speech given by someone who kayaked around the Antarctica.) The speech was awe-inspiring and humbling, but afterwards, I returned home unaffected and thought nothing more of it.

However, not so for Roger. The next day in his office, the conversation continued. He had not forgotten.

He asked me, "How adventurous are you?"

(After reading a few of my stories, dear reader, you can imagine how puffed up I got with pride in order to answer this question appropriately.)

"I would imagine, quite adventurous," I answered.

"Great! How do you feel about climbing Mount Everest? We are going to Base Camp in a few months and I am gathering a crew. Are you interested?"

It is worth mentioning that Roger is a man in his 70s. 74 to be exact. This "old" man questioned my sense of adventure and then threw down the gauntlet: climbing the almighty Everest.

The flag waved red. The glove was slammed to the floor. The fencer back stepped, raising his saber épée. His eyebrow lifted in question, waiting for my reply.

Damn right, I said yes.

"Sign me up. What do you need and how do we make this happen?" I was in. Body and soul.

———

Ok. Maybe more soul than body. And maybe more pride than soul.

I had a list of things to purchase. That I could do. Easy peezy and done. (Shopping is my jam. And looking the part is essential.) I might not have hiked a hill but I was going to look like I had just come down from the Matterhorn. (I exaggerate. I was going to look more like I had just climbed Mont Blanc. Fashion is important. Because impressing people with brand names is really what counts when you are cold, wet, tired and have not showered in days.)

Roger had told me a few things to do in advance of the trip. He said that the higher we climb, the less oxygen there is. Everyone reacts differently to it. If we were to get altitude sickness, then we should listen to our body and respect it. People have died from altitude sickness.

He also suggested that I hike and run a bit in order to prepare the body. I looked at him and sighed. Run? I hate running. Is there anyway I get up the mountain without exertion? No? Ok, memo to self: must hike on own volition with own body.

———

That weekend, I told my friends of my latest "mission impossible". Their response was to remind me of the time I registered to run the New York City marathon and ended up flying to New York and doing a Sex and City restaurant and bar marathon instead. It was far more fun and no running was necessary.

But this was not something I could get around. Luckily for me, I had a boyfriend at the time who was not opposed to outdoor sex, ergo merging what I hated with what I love. Sex on the top. It was like a well-deserved dessert. It was the kind of practice I liked. Thus when it came to D-Day, the extent of my training was hiking a few hills, having sex at the summit, and then walking down. Not forgetting the cigarettes, before and after the "hike".

Furthermore, I did not need to practice that much because I was already used to not breathing well. I was a smoker. Same, same but different.

I was perfectly prepared. A poster boy for National Geographic.

Not.

———

The average, normal thinking, responsible adult would be blasting me by now. Don't worry, reader. That is what my friends are for. Maturity in times of irresponsibility. But after several warnings, they still let me go. Not for fear of my health, but knowing that nothing stops me.

The first thing I needed to do at the airport was to find out where Kathmandu is. And then check in, and get to the gate. I was excited to meet the team that I'd be with for the next 2 weeks.

Looking around, I came to the quick conclusion that this was no longer a silly game for a silly princess. I was unprepared. I was seriously unprepared. They looked like they had hiked Mont Blanc, Matterhorn, and Denali. During the weekend. Last weekend. Every weekend.

I also noted that I was one of the youngest. We were between the ages of 35 and 75. From all walks of life. None of us knew each other; it was a completely random group of ragamuffin school teachers, insurance brokers, writers. Each of us were pseudo-hikers and bona fide adventurers.

As I clocked their ages, especially those in their 70's, I thought to myself: this is good. I will not be last. The one dragging behind.

If I die, someone will be there to revive me.

Preparation is not my strong suit. Drama is, darling.

———

Our flight to Kathmandu was uneventful, which means the plane worked. However, all snark aside, coming to the magical place of Kathmandu was a dream come true for me. Since we arrived late at night, we did not see any of the city but went straight to bed. However, the next morning, I was up early. It was a phenomenal first day, wandering through the streets, meeting the people, praying in the temples, observing with gratitude the lush culture of the Nepalese.

After exiting a temple, I saw children playing in a pool of water and decided to join them, splashing around. I got completely wet. It was so much fun to share in their freedom and the joy of the moment.

By the time I got back to the hotel, my attitude had changed regarding this trip. I knew that this was not just a hike up a mountain. I knew that this was not a tourist vacation in the Himalayas. I knew that this was a journey that would be significant. How? I did not know. But I was ready for the 'climb'.

Later that evening, we gathered for a meal at a local restaurant. For some reason, the hostess placed her thumb on my forehead, leaving a stamp made of orange powder. It most probably was meant for touristic reasons, but I felt anointed in a way.

The plane left for Lukla early the next morning. As we were walking onto the tarmac, we stopped in our tracks. A pilot was kneeling before the plane, brushing the steps with goat's blood for good luck. This was a different kind of 'anointing'.

Ok... Good luck is good to have. I am not so sure about the strength of fighting evil spirits by the blood of goats. But if it gave the pilot the confidence he needed to navigate the ragged peaks of the Himalayas, then I was: "Amen, brother. Let me help."

We strapped in and our small twin engine plane took off. I spent the entire time looking out the window as we weaved through the peaks above the clouds. It was magical. And then I saw the reason for the pilot's concern. We turned the corner and started to descend into Lukla. To say that it was a small runway would be an understatement. I can knit longer sweaters than this runway. And this is where the pilot needed to land. On this thumbtack of a cement clinging to the side of a cliff, in the mountains of the Himalayas.

God bless goat's blood.

Already after the first day of our climb, our climbing pack had already broken up into different groups. Each one keeping a different pace. And to my surprise I was in the front part of the climbing tribe.

For those of you who have been worried about my pride, fear not. My pride was somewhat salvaged. For although I was in the front part of the group; I was still behind four men that were 74, 72, 71, and 69 years old. Colonel Brumhill was naturally in front. These men (twice my age) were running up the mountain. I might have been out of breath, but I was not going to be out-paced by men that were older than my parents. I was determined to keep up.

Oh, silly pride.

I joke but I had to tip my hat in sincere respect. They were inspirational. Not just because of their age, but because of the fantastic stories and insights they shared along the way. I was in great company. I really was.

I will save my reflections of our climb for another chapter, one more designed to touch the heart and build pillars of the soul. It will be for another time that I will go into the details of our walk, the scenery, and the people. I was humbled by the hospitality of the Nepalese people; they give even though they have nothing. I took part in the prayers at the Buddhist monastery and numerous shrines along the way. I will recount the dream-like walks through forests and under canopies of prayer flags. These images will forever stay with me. At another time I shall reflect on the heart to heart conversations in the dark nights, or of the banter shared while we struggled with our sighs as we climbed. I will tell another time of the deep breaths needed to push through upwards. Or the moment that I first saw the peak of the mighty Mount Everest. And the huge smile I had. All that, I will save that for another time. It would take a book in itself. And justifiably so.

For we walked amongst the clouds. In the Himalayas. With every minute and every step I was struck by how amazing it was. That I was actually there. Climbing Everest. I had actually made myself dumbstruck. It was supremely humbling. I kneeled before the majesty that is Nepal, that are the Himalayas, that is the world of Everest.

———

The lessons were numerous: preparation (I know you will smile at that one), persistence, gratitude, and the ability to stand still while walking. I was nowhere else but there. I could not be. It was impossible not to be completely present in conversation.

Moreover, the most important lessons were taught by the people of Nepal: humility, strength, and happiness. The Nepalese are always smiling. I was confused at first, but then why I was confused? Isn't that supposed to be the norm? If those people, who live outside 1st world existence, with nothing, if these people are always smiling, then I have no reason not to. I was chastened.

What was also awe-inspiring was their strength. The guides, the sherpas were incredibly strong. They ran up the "damn mountain" every day, with bags and food on their back. I was in awe. They ran up the mountain of Everest as if it were flat land, grass plains.

And they do it smiling.

Yes, I was humbled with the numerous lessons I was being taught.

But there was more for me to learn.

At times, we would walk single file and speaking would not be possible. Then, the memories of unresolved discussion and remnants of broken hearts would rise to the surface. What became clear was that each of us would be transported into a world of thought and reflection, often difficult to digest. Sometimes, it would be even harder to snap back and join the social interactions of the group.

One night, the Colonel addressed us newbies, seeing the struggle on our faces and anticipating the mental journey of Everest.

"Everest is not always a mountain in the Himalayas. To those of who struggling with your ghosts, leave them on the mountain," he said.

A small bomb of eureka went off, a soothing balm to the torture I had been giving my soul. Leave it on the mountain. And as I continued to climb, I left mental gravestones along the way, taking one ghost of burden after another to their final resting place: on the mountain.

By the time we were crossing the 5000 meter mark, about to climb to Base Camp, I was more than physically tired, I was soul tired, in tatters. The next 24 hours would be brutal. Where do you go when you have nothing left? I was empty. Where do you find the strength? Nothing prepared me or could have ever have prepared me. I had never experienced this.

And of course this would be the time when my altitude sickness would kick in. Goddamn cigarettes.

I was not the only one that suffered from altitude sickness.

Many were affected. Some could not continue on, hesitant to jeopardize their health, wisely listening to their bodies.

The rest of us continued on, but we were no longer climbing as a group. Most of us turned inwards, choosing our own pace instead of that of the pack. It took concentration to climb. My biggest chore was trying to resist resting for long periods of time. Boulders started to look like comfortable pillows. But I knew I was never going to get to Base Camp if I did not continue. Base Camp was not going to come to me.

And so I took one step at time. One foot in front of another. When I did stop, it would be to appreciate the glaciers we crossed and the peak we were about to meet.

All thought was gone. Only determination. And then suddenly, there was faith. The humble and kind version. The ghosts were gone and I was full of gratitude for everything that had been given me, the experiences I had lived, and the opportunities offered.

I continued on through the ice, to meet my Everest, in prayer: Thank you. Thank you. Thank you. The mantra, the focus, the journey enabled me to finally reach my goal: Base Camp. With a humbled and grateful heart. With a tired but peaceful soul.

Interestingly enough, each of us had chosen a different mantra. One counted bottles of beer on the wall. Literally. One friend tried to list all the countries in the world while another joined in trying to list all the capitals. Not everyone shared what their source of strength was or what mantra which kept him going. I imagine that some were slightly more profound. It was a vulnerable time for all.

Climbing had become more than another boastful story to tell while sitting around a campfire. It had become a journey of the heart and soul.

What was the inspiration for my mantra? I believe it was a combination: personal faith, walking for days beneath canopies of prayer flags, chiming in with Buddhist monks along the way, twirling the prayer wheels lining the monasteries. It could also be the influence of a friend of mine, who after learning he was HIV positive, starts every morning in gratitude, and makes every step of his feet to represent his thanks: his left foot is "thank" and his right foot: "you".

And as I descended, I continued my prayer. Thank. You. Thank. You.

Thank you for this challenge.
Thank you for this opportunity.
Thank you for this life.

———

On the way down, conversations became lighter along with our steps and our hearts. I was not the only one who left something on the mountain. Everest had given us all something. We all had something to take away. For some, it was the sense of accomplishment. For others, it was the conversations that had transpired. Others with the feeling that they had nothing more to prove, that they were good in their own skin. We all had fresh memories of battles won, physical and spiritual alike. A natural bonding of friendship had taken place, founded in our experience and cemented with our new found love of Nepal and her people.

And me? Well. For me, it was all of the above and more. When the dust settled and I came back home, what did I do?

I opened up the map of the world to find other mountains to climb. I was truly born again. An Everest convert. Since Nepal, I have climbed many more mountains.

That being said, it was not a 180 change. I am not a complete convert. I still prefer sex to hiking. Call me a snob but when others invite me for a Saturday afternoon hike, I wave them off with: "You climb your ant hill. I only climb mountains." (Don't worry, I do receive a good amount of abuse for that comment. But I can't help myself...)

However, to be honest, even though I still cannot stand hiking for the sake of "fresh air", every once in awhile, I look to the peaks and pray:

Give me my resting place.
Give me my torture.
Give me my challenge.
Give me my nirvana.
Give me my prayer.

Give me a mountain to climb.

——————

Lagniappe

Dal Bhat
40 minutes

1½ cups uncooked rice
1 cup dry lentils
1 onion
3 cloves garlic
1 tablespoon olive oil

1 can tomatoes
⅓ cup cilantro
1 lime
1 red chili

Season: salt, cumin, coriander, tumeric, cayenne, pepper

1. Begin cooking the rice. (2 cups water to 1 cup rice ratio)

2. Heat oil in a pan over medium heat, add onion and garlic. Sauté until soft.

3. Add lentils for 2 minutes before adding 3 cups of water to let cook.

4. After 15 minutes, add the spices to taste, tomatoes, and more water if it looks dry.

5. Simmer until lentils are cooked and the flavors have blended to taste.

6. Take off the stove and add cilantro.

7. By this time, the rice is cooked. Serve with lime wedges, sliced chilies, and more cilantro.

I had this a lot on the trek, almost always with water or black tea with lots and lots of sugar. (Fortification for any "mountain" you need to climb.) However, at home, away from being the healthier version of myself, I prefer my curries with a bottle of cold beer.

"May you live all the
days of your life."

Jonathan Swift

SPEAKING WITH THE DOLPHINS

Sudan

The water was warm. And I loved to swim. I was in heaven.

"How refreshing," I thought to myself as I pushed further out through the waves, away from the shore.

My two friends were right behind me, shouting how wonderful it was to be in the water. Especially after almost 12 hours in the car riding through the desert. Caked with dust and fatigued to the bone, with tempers fraying, we made a mutual executive decision to stop for the night and set up camp.

And wonders of wonders, the road we were on led us to this remote beach, untouched and uninhabited. It looked out on a secluded bay leading out to the Red Sea. We felt welcomed by this twist of fate giving us the best resting place one could ever imagine.

Beach, sunset, sea. Who could ask for more? Besides directions of course, but our anxiety was soon forgotten after we shook off our shoes, sunk our toes into the hot sand and ran into the water.

Flipping to my back, I started to float, taking it all in. What a sight it was. Not a cloud in the sky. Not a speck of white. Just color. The sun was setting on the horizon, flooding the sky with a blistering red and orange. The emerald green of the Red Sea stretched out further that the eye could see, way passed the setting sun on the horizon.

It was if we had painted it all. Scratch that. No one would ever be able to paint this because it was so perfect.

And for us, it was a balm for the soul: a glorious ending to a horrible couple of days.

As I moved the water, I soaked up the sensations: the feeling of tiredness and trial had been replaced by one of happiness and wonder. All of a sudden, I felt something touch my feet. I immediately flipped to my back, looking around for the boys to see if it was them playing underwater. Both of them were far from me. And I since I could see them, I knew they weren't playing games. Taking a deep breath, I dove and did not see anything.

Surfacing, I looked around and shrugged it off, continuing to swim. And then I felt it again. I dove again and still nothing. This was weird. All I saw was the ocean floor.

Coming up for air again, I turned on my back and half-kicking and half-floating, looking up at the blood orange sky.

Whoosh!

This huge grey mass came out of the water on my left, crossed over me, and dove back down. It happened so fast that I wasn't sure if it was real. I held my breath and crossed my fingers.

Straightening up, I yelled over to the boys: "Did you see that? What was that?"

I looked at them and their jaws were open in awe.

Paul shouted, "Christina, look!" He pointed to the horizon.

Dolphins. And more dolphins. They were everywhere. Lots of them.

Jumping out the sea and back in. Backflipping. We were surrounded by them. There were dolphins jumping everywhere - not one or two, but more than twenty. It was incredible.

I reached out my hand to feel them, chasing them in the water. I wanted to play too, completely in awe of the gift to connect with this glorious creature. Let me rephrase: creatures.

We swam with them, laughing when we surfaced before diving again to play. I didn't know how dolphins talked but I imagined it was like a sonar system. So, I tried to mimic "dolphin speak" when I was underwater. Silly, I know, but I felt an undeniable connection, joy, and wonder.

I came up for air, stretched up my hand and felt the underbelly of one as it flew over my head.

Wow. Wow.

Magic.

They surrounded us. Playing, swimming, jumping. Before long, they were on their way chasing the sun which was busy setting on the horizon.

I will never forget the image and emotion, being submerged in delight and connection with this world. The kind of experience which is completely unexpected: to be on a barren beach, swimming in emerald waters, under a fuschia sky. And the wonder and joy goes into overdrive as I personally share the aqua playground with a family of dolphins.

As they left, I was filled with peace, happiness and awe. Grateful for this wonder-filled world that we live in.

I wish that you experience the bliss of playing with dolphins, at least once in your life.

Yes, I wish this for you.

———————

Lagniappe

Yoghurt and Tahini Dip
120 seconds

After being introduced to this dish, it has become one of my staples. Easy as 1,2,3. Great with vegetables or pita bread. More or less, it is the most practical and tasty snack evah.

⅔ cup tahini
⅔ cup plain nonfat yogurt
3 cloves garlic, minced
2 lemon, juiced
2 tablespoons fresh parsley, chopped
Season: salt and pepper

1. Mix the dry.

2. Add the wet, slowly. Mix well. It is supposed to be like cream.

3. Sprinkle, season and serve. It really is that easy.

Have something cool and refreshing: ice tea, white wine, beer... something you would have sitting on a beach, watching the dolphins play in the sunset.

"Save a horse,
ride a cowboy"

Big Kenny & John Rich

Hijacking Automobiles
Central America

Option A: Stay and take my chances of surviving the night. Option B: Hijack the car.

Hmmmmm. Live or die? Yup, I choose life. Life again and again. Much better than getting gang raped and beaten. Truth or dare? Yup. Still the same answer.

Life. Always.

This was no drinking game. This was real life. And, I was in a situation that had gotten waaaay out of hand. An interview gone wrong. A business deal with some pretty unhappy customers. Believe me "safe spaces" were nowhere to be found.

I am the hero of my story and I am going to get myself out of this mess.

Or die trying.

It is the middle of the night. Pitch black night. Where you could almost eat the dark, it was so dense. Probably because we are in the jungle. Not even the crickets and snakes are awake. Everyone is asleep.

Which is good for me, I wanted everyone to stay asleep.

While I steal their car.

Simplezz.

Now, there is a tiny, itsy, bitsy, small problem.

I know nothing about cars.

Nada. Niet. Zilch.

I do not know how to change a tire or where to fill the oil. All I know is summarized in three things: how to fill the gas, how the radio works and where the gas and the brakes are. More than that...well, nope - I do not know more than that.

This time my life depends on it. So, when there is a will there is a way. I am not going to freak out. Instead, I am going to hijack this old Mercedes that belongs to the 'Chefe'. Wild guess: he is not going to be happy when he sees that it is gone.

But let's face it. No matter what I did was he going to be happy. He might react strongly to me taking his car though.

I was not alone. I had Rachel, my assistant, with me. There were two lives on the line here. She was too young to get involved in this mess, but I have a soft spot for those who want to learn on the job and never give up. What she does not have in experience to make better informed decisions, she makes up for being present and making it happen. Guts and gutso. My kind of magic.

And we needed magic here. The only problem was that she knew as much as I did about cars. Zero times zero is still zero.

We needed a win. Anything.

Turning to her, I said, " Know anything about hijacking cars?"

Shocked, she replied, "What? You can't be serious? You are not going to steal his car! He is going to kill us!"

"He is going to kill us anyway, honey. And I have a penchant for consensual sex. Rape, not so much," I replied.

"Besides, I will bring the car back."

Scratch that. I was never coming back here. She did not know that. I told myself that I would not completely steal the car but would 'borrow' it. For a while.

Or forever. The jury was still out.

I lifted all the handles of the car, hoping, to see if any of my prayers would be answered. Not so easy. Apparently, God was asleep, too. It was all up to me.

I bent down and grabbed a rock. Tap. Tap. Smash!

The crashing of glass was contained on the driver's side. I tried to be as quiet as possible. Rachel was less quiet. She was obviously set against my 'borrowing' the car.

"You cannot do this!" she whispered loudly. In my opinion, it was the same as sounding an alarm to notify our future-would-be-captors of our whereabouts and our intent to escape.

And I was not having any of this. Nope. Not tonight. Mutiny of any kind was just not on any menu. It was not in my dictionary. And I was going to erase it from hers.

"Snap out of it! Get it together. We are getting out of here. Or you can stay here and go back inside. Your choice. But you are either with me - and quiet - or not. I am trying to save both of our lives. Your choice if you want to save yours. But you will not put my life in jeopardy because you would rather sacrifice both our lives because you do not want to borrow a car! It ain't happening. So, get with it!" I finished shaking her arms.

I turned to lean over the car door to open it from the inside. Gently wiping the glass off the seat, I slid in. By this time, I was channeling my inner Macgyver. What would he do? I have seen cars being jacked all the time in the movies and they always pulled the bottom part of the steering wheel off in order to access the wires.

Cool. I can do that. Using my high heel shoes and the rock, I started pulling on the plastic. I got so far as to get a good grip on it and bracing both my feet against the dashboard. And pulled.

And pulled.

It gave way. Came loose. Then off.

Yes! I sighed and exhaled. Good. This was working. We were far from getting on the road but this was a good sign. At least, I took it as an affirmation. One thing at a time.

Now, what would Macgyver do next? Looking at the wires hanging down, my fleeting moment of pride and hope started strangling again; oxygen of hope was disappearing in view of the reality I was looking at. It looked like a bowl of pasta - made of wires. In every single color. All mixed up. I had no idea which one was which. We were going to be here for a while if I didn't figure this out soon.

And being here for a while did not really coincide with my plans for living.

Rachel, standing over me, shining the light from her phone, whispered, "What do the directions say? I mean, what does it say in the manual?"

She had gotten with the program. And big time. Thank God.

I smiled at her. "You are so smart. That is a great idea." Apparently, that was all she needed for the panic to recede. I could see her body relax as she morphed into a pirate before my eyes. Her guts and gutso was back. Encouraged by what I saw, I started to relax a bit. The two of us were going to get out of here.

Oh yeahhhhh.

Reaching over to the glove compartment, I took out the manual, handing it to her to read while I started separating the wires into groups. From what I remembered (from watching all the hundreds of movies) was that the battery is pretty important to start the car. The second part I remembered was that you need to spark two wires together. But which wires? Which one was the battery? And which wire was the spark? Not knowing the answer, I turned to Rachel for help.

"Which one is the ignition and which one is the battery?" I asked.

"Yellow is battery. And red is ignition." She put the phone light closer to the wires.

Now, I also know there always being a spark, a literal spark. Which meant that I had to take the wires out and strip them, since I knew they had to be live to make the car start.

God bless Hollywood action movies. Seriously. I love you, Hollywood.

"Please, please," I mantra-prayed while stripping the wires. We had been out in the dark for a while. My nervousness was not abating, fully aware that time was not my friend here. We needed to get away.

Next step was to actually start the car. This meant tapping them to imitate the ignition.

Spark. Pszzt. The electricity sparked.

Rachel was praying. I was holding my breath.

After a few tries, the car started.

My head rested on the dashboard. Oh holy hell, that was close. The adrenaline rush was sweeping.

Rachel fist pumped. And then ran around in circles, making a little dance. I was smiling, riding the wave of amazement. This was incredible. I could not believe that it worked.

"Rachel! Get in!" I said. She ran around the car and got in the other side.

We had gotten the car started but the steering wheel would not budge. You have got to be kidding me. Really, fate? This is how it ends? Get so close but still so far. Banging the car, I sighed and resolved to find a way.

Because - no. Just no. We were not giving up. There has got to be a way to force the wheel to turn. How about a little bit of brute strength. Since, there was no way I was going take my foot of the gas, or risk doing so, I asked Rachel to get out and help me turn the wheel. Four arms are better than two.

She ran around again and grabbed the wheel. The two of us jerked, swearing and cussing, as quietly as we could. We were exasperated, frustrated but determined.

And then we heard a snap. The steering wheel moved.

Oh yeahhhhh.

Smiling big time to myself, Rachel did another happy dance in the middle of the road before she ran around the car to get in again.

Closing the door, we looked at each other with huge grins and silently high fived. I turned the car into the road and started driving back to the city, away from the danger we were literally escaping.

I kept on praying gratitude. God definitely was not asleep. That was so close.

Too close.

Rachel was biting her fist because she wanted to scream in victory that we had actually hotwired a car. I wanted to scream that we were driving home, away from danger and away from the worst of tragedies. We were both holding it together to keep quiet, until we were far away from any human ears.

Breaths were held until we got onto the main road when we let go and screamed at the top of our lungs. Yes! Over and over again. Yes. There was jumping in our seats and sitting dancing moves all round, singing to the top of our lungs. Our victory was not only escaping the danger but also making it happen. I mean come on, it is a huge feat: hotwiring a car when all you know is to how turn radio channels.

We were proud.

"I never felt like a badass before. It feels good." Rachel said as she looked out the window, watching the country landscape as we went speeding by.

Lighting a cigarette, I exhaled. For the first time in hours.

Amen. That it did.

That it did.

Lagniappe

This story of badassery does not call for a meal which takes time ergo, my first suggestion would be for a shot of your favorite tequila with lime along with a bowl of guacamole and chips. You cannot beat that. For those that like their tequila, try having it with orange wedges, or with chili chocolate for dessert.

Try this following recipe as well. It is equally badass.

Ginger, Lemon, and Garlic Swordfish Steak

30 minutes (or more depending on how much tequila you drink while making it)

Grill: High

2½ cm ginger root, peeled and finely chopped
2 garlic cloves, crushed
Juice of 1 lemon
2 spring onions, chopped
1 red chili, deseeded and finely chopped
2 tablespoons olive oil
4 swordfish steaks

1. Put ginger and garlic into a small bowl and mix to form a paste.
2. Add the lemon juice, spring onions, chili and oil and then mix again.
3. Coat the swordfish steaks with the mixture and leave to marinate for 15 minutes.
4. Grill on high heat for 5 to 6 minutes, turning once.

Serve with marinade drizzled, potatoes, lime wedges.... And tequila.

"As long as you live, keep learning how to live."

Seneca

PHOENIX IN PARIS

France

The story I tell here is not crazy or humourous. It is not amazing. There is no tragedy or comedy. There is no life changing event. It is a story of what happens to you when you think nothing is going on. And the glorious adventure that that is.

Mine took place in Paris. Lucky me. Some cities are true to their reputation. Paris is one, if not the city, that holds true to all the songs, stories, myths and legends. Paris truly is a moveable feast.

There is an aura about this city. It is the home to where the kings played polo and the peasants revolted. It is home to the authors, painters, philosophers whom we have marveled at throughout the centuries. There is a reason Paris is so inspiring. I have never turned a corner without being awestruck by its beauty. One continually walks as if on a movie set or captured in a postcard: the majestic architecture of the buildings, bathing in the white gold sun, the cobbled streets, the trees lining the sidewalks, gracing every cafe. The hum of conversations and the perfume of the hanging flowers during the summer are sensations caught in my memories as I stroll beneath the bridges of locks while gazing upon the halo of Notre Dame. A kaleidoscope of colors is brought on by the sunset, visualized in surround sound, mirrored on the waters of the Seine as she rolls away another day.

I have a confession to make: I didn't come to Paris for the city. I did not come as a tourist. I came for a job. What started out as a search in jest, choosing between Paris, Rome or Madrid, depending on my language capabilities, took a serious turn after surviving cancer. I was recovering from chemotherapy and wanted to be closer to family. Through a series of events, I left my home, my Hong Kong and set off to become a Parisienne.

Visiting Paris is intoxicating while living in Paris is quite another coupe de champagne. It is not easy; Paris makes you work to be loved by her. One of the many reasons why I call her my mistress. In Paris, there is no welcome committee, no congregation of world travelers, or expats to explain, commiserate, meet, greet, laugh and cry with. For the first time, in a very long time, I felt stranded without my tribe.

Away from the maddening crowd, Paris invites you to spend time alone at cafes, thinking into space, smoking cigarettes while watching the runway of life. Soon enough my routine would be work-filled days followed by long walks at night.

This change made me stop. To stop planning ahead and appreciate the now. To reflect. To dream. To break it down and build it up again. To be present.

The purist in me wanted to be one with the philosophers of old, reaching answers to quantum physics of thought, found only through the pain of loneliness while surrounded by beauty. Hours, days, and nights spent walking the empty streets forced me to settle one memory after another, answering the questions that tripped on the ones before. The mind hurt, the heart broke again, and the soul was fatigued.

Cleaning house of the spirit was never meant to be easy. At times, surgery might be required. In my case, I had started this journey a few times before, in Nepal, in Algeria but I had never finished getting off the 'operating table'. Now, when everything had come to a halt, the time for healing became more important than ever. Furthermore, I had to reckon with something that I had previously been unfamiliar with.

Fear.

I had reported on war and seen death and human tragedy for years. I was never fearful. I was the one that tapped danced on land mines and stopped planes in their tracks. Death was something that happened to *other* people, not me. What I realized was that cancer had found the chink in my armor. I was vulnerable.

I was not comfortable with this concept. Furthermore, I refused to be a victim. That fear created doubt which turned into depression. I could not understand why I was no longer fearless. How is it possible to be both fearless and vulnerable?

I was missing something and I did not know what it was. And so the battle with depression raged on.

The long days at work left only the nights available to heal. The insomnia consoled me, leaving me awake, forcing me to deal with my reality. During those hours, I knew I was not alone. Because I had Paris. Her streets after midnight beckoned, asking me to keep her company while everyone else was asleep.

Surrounded by the blanket of midnight, underneath her starry skies, I walked her frozen pathways. It is then, during those early hours, that I came to peace with the rush of life, the life I had lived, and the choices I made.

Moreover, I started to remember. The stories of the Algerian women who got up to dance, the Russians who sang as the plane was on fire, and the tsunami of tragedy turned into one of love. I remembered the determination to survive in the dark in Mexico, and those who battled the rapids in Africa, raced the cliffs in Turkey, or polished bombs in the Solomon Islands. I found love for a country in the fruit farmer in Cuba, gratitude for time in Manila, the joy of being present with the dolphins in Sudan or the happiness in finding life fight for itself in the Sahara. I remembered how precious family time is over pizza, and bowed my head in appreciation as I recognized the fearlessness it takes to fall in love. I remembered all these amazing wonderful experiences and more.

And remembering it all, I found what I was "missing". It was something more than being fearless. All my stories and all my travels had one common denominator: Courage. The kind it takes to live, laugh, and love *despite* the fear. To love life. To live life. To maximize it.

———————

My hands and feet were usually ice-cold by the time I would get home. But I didn't mind, my soul was grateful, and my heart was lighter.

During those wee small hours of the morning, multiple decisions were made for the next chapter of my life. Especially the promise to myself that I have three choices every morning: I can be fearless. I can be courageous. And if that fails: I can just be bad-ass.

And so a few hours later when the sun came up the next day, I rose again to fight another battle, to chase another dream, but this time it was different.

This time I was the dream.

Life was not going to happen to me.

I was going to happen to life.

Bring it on.

Bring it all on.

══════════

Lagniappe

Champagne, wine: pick your color.

Wine and cheese. C'est tout.

If you are not in love with food and wine when you get to Paris, you will be by the time you leave. It truly is a moveable feast. The education that I got in food and wine is unsurpassable and what a joy to learn it all. Who can turn down the opportunity to learn when your homework is to eat and drink? I clearly stepped up to the plate, "reluctant", twisted my rubber arm and am now the proud owner of a diploma. (I am so proud of this; I had to tell you about it.)

One of the first lessons I learned was to slow down and enjoy. The most expensive meal can seem tasteless if rushed, and the cheapest meal divine if savoured. Start with taking time with cheese and wine. There is no reason to rush such a joyous activity.

I believe there are great cheese and fabulous wines out there which do not break the bank. For less than 10 euros, you can get a feast in France. If you melt certain cheeses (camembert) in the oven, they become a thing of the gods.

Chop shallots and saute them together with a few mushrooms in butter and cognac. Season it with a bit of salt and shake of pepper before covering the melted camembert.

Eat it with a piece of warm fresh baguette. I swear you will die and go to heaven. Straight to heaven. 7th.

And of course, do not forget to enjoy it with a glass of red wine. Or a glass of champagne, if you were to twist my rubber arm.

La vie est belle!

"Give a man a fish, he eats for a day. Teach him how to fish, he eats forever."

Proverb

BLAME IT ON PARIS: MISSION TO MAXIMIZE

I believe there is no greater adventure than this life. So many people just exist. But I want you to maximize life. To carpe every diem. Now, I could give you a fish (this book) and you could eat for a day. Or I could teach you how to fish and give you a fishing pole.

During those walks in Paris, I decided to "stop a plane" and make good on what I believe. I want that you experience the magic of travel, whether you are student living with college loans, a solo traveler discovering your hidden hero, the family wanting to explore despite mortgages and school fees, or the baby boomer wanting to see fireworks all over the world.

This is the spark that created GenieMe: a tool kit, a lifestyle, a mission to maximize. Parts of the maximizing tool kit are launching now: GenieMe Travel App (www.geniemetravelapp.com) is on the App store in a few weeks as is 24 Hour Weekend website, 24hourweekend.com. If you want to get away or if you want to stay at home, you can travel...you'll see. Check them out. They are awesome.

Stay tuned at geniemetravelapp.com or @geniemetravel on social for everything else that is coming down the pipe, especially the YouTube channel. Life is not just about the destination but about the journey. At GenieMe, we think it is both. And we want it all. It is going to be so much fun...

And this is only the beginning...

One final note, this book is the first book in a series. Volume 2 is already in the works. But next time, I will do something different; I will add your travel stories of how you maximized life and made it magic. If you want to share them, please send them to me. And... if your story is chosen for Volume 2, then I will pay for any flight you find on GenieMe. Anywhere in the world.

For real. No joke. I seriously want you to travel. To maximize life. That is my mission.

Blame Paris if you want to.

————

christina@geniemetravelapp.com / @geniemetravel

#maximizelife

————

Congratulations!

Today is your day.

You're off to Great Places!

You're off and away!

You have brains in your head.

You have feet in your shoes.

You can steer yourself

any direction you choose.

Dr. Seuss, excerpt from
"Oh, The Places You Will Go"

VOLUME 2

About the Author

Christina is a Swedish American author, entrepreneur, and public speaker. Formerly an award winning journalist, managing director of one of the largest global banks, and successful seed philanthropist, Christina is now founder and CEO of GenieMe Technologies Inc., a tech company dedicated to maximizing life. A global nomad, Christina has worked and lived extensively in Africa, Asia, Americas, Europe, and the Middle East. She speaks 11 languages.

22386923R00188

Printed in Great Britain
by Amazon